A Holly Jolly Christmas

KATIE MONTINARO

Wildflower Publishing

ISBN: 978-0-6450918-2-3 (paperback)

Editor: Laura Boon

Cover art and design: Melody Jeffries

For Mum,
My first reader, fellow bookworm and lover of all things Christmas.

Chapter One

Sunday, 19th December – 6 days to go

Do you know why they never make holiday movies or write Christmas-themed books about a Christmas Down Under? I do. It's because there is absolutely nothing romantic about sweat dripping from your back, crack and thighs while you swat away flies under the summer sun. Nothing. At. All. A white Christmas, however, is all about the romance; it encourages you to snuggle up with a loved one under a soft blanket or to drink hot chocolate by the fire whilst snow falls outside. If anyone tries to get close to me on Christmas Day, in this heat, they're likely to cop a fly swatter to the head.

As a born and bred Melbourne girl, I'm used to surviving all four seasons in one day. Although December is technically the start of our summer, it doesn't really get hot until February. Even then, it takes all day to reach the top predicted temperature for all of an hour or two before cooling off by nightfall. Not this year, though. This year we are experiencing an unseasonably hot December (thanks global warming!) and in these six days leading up to Christmas, there is no end in sight for this ridiculous heat wave.

To top things off, my house has evaporative cooling. So you know, basically no cooling whatsoever. I stopped using the cooling three days ago when the wooden floorboards of my house essentially turned into a water park from the humidity. Oh, did I forget to mention that? Yeah, Melbourne doesn't *do* dry heat. We do humid heat. Fun! So not only am I sweating like a pig, but my hair also looks like Season 9 Monica at the palaeontologists' convention in Barbados. I've tamed the wild beast for now, throwing it up in a bun on top of my head as I wait for an iced coffee at my favourite little cafe by the beach.

"Holly? Holly Jolly?" Jean-Luc calls my name with a huge smile.

That's me. Since learning my surname, Jean-Luc and his husband (and pastry chef extraordinaire, Pierre) has never once passed up the opportunity to use it in full - especially at this time of the year. My parents thought that having a child born on Christmas Eve was too good an opportunity to pass up to give their newborn a stupid name. They told me years later that it was because I was their little Christmas miracle. Tell that to my brother, Jesse. He wanted a bike. Worst. Christmas. Ever. It has taken him a long time to get over that one. But this year, I am going to deliver the Best. Christmas. Ever. So he can finally stop whinging at me for the month of December each and every year.

I take my drink from Jean-Luc which most definitely wasn't the small I ordered. I open my mouth to say something, but he speaks first.

"I upgraded for you," he says with that thick French accent that we all enjoy way too much.

With a wink, the silver fox hands me a box of French desserts full of cream, sugar and pastry. I thank him and wish him and his husband a Merry Christmas, thankful that someone has my back today. The moment I ordered a small, iced coffee I instantly regretted not making it a large. Jean-Luc must have sensed my need for something to get me through the next couple of *Delilah-ful* hours. Maybe he has already encountered her today? It wouldn't surprise me in the slightest if she had checked the order to ensure it was ready. Or if she checked to see if I had forgotten the one task, she assigned me. As I step out of the cool cafe into the street, a wave of heat hits me like an oven door opening. It is most unusual for it to already be this hot, this early in the morning. I take my time walking up the street towards my parent's home. I browse a few overpriced shop windows and dodge a few mums with prams before conceding that it is far too hot to be outside any longer.

Mum and Dad live in a deceptively opulent two-story town house opposite the water at Safety Beach. It's quiet down this end as most people drive through on their way to Dromana or Sorrento - the glamorous parts of the Peninsula for out of town-ers. And I guess that's just the way the locals like it. Close enough to the beach without all the crowds, especially during summer. My parent's house has undergone major renovations over the last five years since Mum became Insta-famous with her lifestyle blog *Delilah-ful*, and now our former family beach shack is a two-story modern marvel that has the most coveted home magazines in the country vying for it to grace the covers of their magazines.

I key in the code on the pad of the pristine white, tall gate that reflects the sun and blinds me in the process. I punch in the wrong code as I cannot see the keypad, and it buzzes at me. I press the call button and hope that Dad picks up. The call button always annoys Mum. She disables it most of the time when she doesn't want visitors.

"Hello," a sweet singsong voice carries down the line.

"Mum?" I question.

"Oh Holly honey, did you get the desserts from Jean-Luc?"

Lucky I did, because I am about one hundred percent sure that she would not buzz me in if I hadn't.

"Yes. Sorry, it's really bright out here. I must have hit the wrong numbers."

She lets out a performance laugh, you know the one your parents do around other people that says, 'Look how carefree I am when my child stuffs up', but you know it's really saying, 'We'll talk about this when they leave'. It catches me off guard.

"Not to worry, sweetheart. Come up."

She buzzes me in, and I skip quickly up the front steps to get inside where I am both relieved and shocked by what I see. "What the..."

"Holly, darling," Mum says sweeping into the room before her eyes have the chance to land on me. She lets out a gasp of her own. "What on earth happened to your hair?"

Her sing-song voice has left the building.

"Yvonne? Yvonne? Have you got a quick minute to do something with Holly's hair?"

Who the heck is Yvonne, and why is she at our family morning tea? And why does she need to touch up my hair? I look around at the sight before me and it is like a white Christmas threw up all over the house. Every possible side table and wall space has been taken over by Christmas ornaments and trinkets. The staircase banisters have been engulfed by fairy-light-dripped wreath runners. Sparkly blue snowflakes strategically hang from the ceiling. A large snow-covered Christmas tree, decorated with ornate ornaments takes over the living room, while twinkling candles adorn the dining room table – which, of course, is styled in blues, silvers and whites. *Delilah-ful's* signature colours. My mouth hangs open as my eyes take in the roomful of unfamiliar faces until they land on my father, sister and brother, each dressed in the same all-white outfit that I had been asked to wear. White linen dresses for the girls in slightly different styles and white linen shirts and shorts for the boys. Someone takes the dessert box out of my hand whilst another glides me to the kitchen stool and forces me to sit. I lost Mum somewhere in between.

"Hmm, this is a huge mess," says a voice behind me as they run their fingers through my mane.

"Huh?"

"I've got some products I can run through it that will help with the frizz and then we can run the irons over it and straighten it out. Should last long enough for the shoot."

The shoot? I feel like I've stepped into the twilight zone.

"Brilliant. Will it take long? We're already running late." Mum reappears.

"About thirty minutes."

"Make it twenty," she orders and someone I guess to be Yvonne nods before tugging a brush through my hair.

The pulling pain reminds me that this is very much *not* a dream.

"Mum, what's going on?"

"Digby? Digby, *darling*, can we start shooting without Holly? Perhaps we could do the close ups of me and of the table settings and decorations?"

A short man dressed in a tight-fitting black tee and pants arrives with a camera in hand. "Of course, *darling*. We can also take some snaps of you and hubby."

My calls for an explanation go unanswered as Mum and Digby busy themselves around the table, laying out Jean-Luc's desserts on the plates. Dad, my brother and my sister sit in the far corner of the kitchen like little children who have been told to stand still so they don't get their outfits dirty. I try and catch their eyes to ask what is going on. My sister, Layla, scrolls mindlessly through her phone, and my brother, Jesse, sits with his arms folded across his chest looking like he'd rather be anywhere else. Dad is the only one who looks my way. When our eyes lock, he comes over.

"Hello, sweetheart."

"Dad, what's going on? I thought we were just having morning tea?"

He sighs. "Your mother has organised all of this," he waves his hands about gesturing to everything in the house, "for her Christmas blog."

He says the last word like it's a dirty one. Dad is an incredibly supportive husband, but he also comes from that generation who believes the only real career is a traditional career, so when Mum said she was quitting her job as a kindy teacher to pursue her "hobby" full time, Dad was sceptical.

"For what? I'm hosting Christmas this year." I'm defensive. "It's my *first* Christmas in my *first* home."

"Unit. You live in a unit." My brother appears beside my dad.

I resist the urge to give him the finger in front of all these people.

"Now, now you two. Your mother has gone to a lot of trouble for today and," he lifts his finger to quieten me as I try to interrupt, "your home is a very lovely little thing, Holly."

"Little, being the word," Jesse remarks.

"Oh bite me, Jesse."

He places his hand to his heart and pretends to be wounded. "Geez, you really got me there, Bart Simpson."

This time I allow my middle finger to release and wave it in his face.

"Can you just...oh stop it." Dad says trying to cover my hand with his. "This is a very important thing for your mother, so we need to support her. She's on the brink of closing in on a big sponsor for her blog, and she's about to hit six hundred thousand likes!"

"Followers," my brother and I say in unison.

"You have no idea what all that means, do you Dad?" Jesse asks, cupping his hand on Dad's shoulder.

"Not in the slightest, but she seems pretty excited by it. And stressed. So can the two of you please get along for the next couple of hours? That's all I ask."

Jesse and I grumble a truce, and it's like we're back to being surly teenagers again instead of two adults in their twenties.

Yvonne continues to tug at my hair, and I have lost all sensation in my scalp. I give into it and watch my mother perform for the camera from afar when I notice her whitened teeth are almost the same shade as the ornaments surrounding her. I giggle to myself. The whole scene before me is surreal. I snap a picture on my phone, but my mother doesn't miss a thing.

"Don't you dare post that, Holly." She points at me before smiling back at Digby and his camera.

I sigh and put my phone down on the bench. I wouldn't dare post anything without her approval. It's something we've gotten used to. We don't post any of the pictures we take of Mum. Instead, she sends us pictures to post that have been perfected by her editor and approved by *Delilah-ful* herself.

"Ready!" Yvonne shouts out to the room and for a brief moment all eyes focus uncomfortably on me.

I shift in my seat as my mother shouts her approval from across the room. "Great. Can we get the family to take their seats at the table? Great. Just find your name tags...that's it, Layla. Great, honey."

Digby shouts directions. "Dennis! Dennis! Can you stand with Delilah at the head of the table? Yep...but...no, if you could just stand slightly behind her and put your hand on her shoulder like this. Yep. Great. Has someone got the turkey?"

There's turkey? I mouth to Jesse who shrugs his shoulders and now seems just as bewildered as I am when a large, glazed turkey on a sliver tray styled with roasted vegetables comes out of the kitchen and lands in front of our parents. Dad looks it over while Mum tells him to stand up straight.

"Is that real?" I ask no-one in particular.

Digby laughs. "First time on a shoot, darl?"

"But...the pastries are real," I say. I'm sure I look as confused as I sound.

"Oh Holly, sweetie," Mum's tone is too highly strung to be sincere, "we need to feed our team something special for giving up their Sunday." She adds in a small laugh that tells the team that I am a complete idiot.

I mean, of course, the people she is paying to do a job *definitely* need to be treated to something for doing their job. Absolutely. I mean, I wonder how other bosses show their gratitude for when people *do* the job they've been *paid* to do. It takes all the will I have not to roll my eyes.

Layla smiles sweetly for the camera and receives Digby's over-the-top praise. "Great. Beautiful. You're a natural Layla, just like your mother. Great!"

This seems to please both Mum and Layla as they flush a little. Jesse rolls his eyes at me from across the table, and I shake my head a little. We've been seated closest to the camera while Layla sits closest to Mum and Dad, all smiling brightly. She flicks her long blonde hair over her shoulder and lets out a little giggle which Digby loves and asks us to all do the same.

"Pretend someone said something funny. That's it. Just a little giggle. Nothing over the top. Holly, just tone it down a bit...yeah great. That's great. Jesse, just lift your chin slightly...yep, more, down a bit though, to the side...yep, perfect. Great."

Snap. Snap. Snap.

I lose track of the number of shots that we have taken as Digby disappears to check them on his computer. The five of us stay in our spots in case we need to take more pictures. I bloody hope not. My cheeks are hurting.

"Isn't this lovely. My team have done a great job in helping me decorate the house for Christmas."

I clear my throat. "I mean, it looks great and all, Mum, but we're not doing Christmas here this year. I'm doing it. It's kinda going to waste."

"I wouldn't say that. We're hosting Christmas Eve dinner," she reminds me, and it irks me just slightly that it is referred to as "Christmas Eve dinner" and not "Holly's birthday dinner". Minor issue that I've been dealing with for almost twenty-six years now.

"Right. So, all of this is for..."

"My Christmas post. I have to have something to post on Christmas Day and the days after."

"But...but...I'm hosting," is all I can manage. Was it just me, or was she not making any sense? This wasn't her Christmas Day.

Christmas Day hadn't happened yet, and it was going to be at my place. My new place. Wouldn't she be posting about that?

"She doesn't think your Christmas will be Instagram worthy." Jesse says as if reading my thoughts. He slides his chair back and slouches down.

"Jesse!" Mum angrily whispers at him.

"Well, it's true. That's why we're all here isn't it? These pictures will be the ones you post to all your followers. A picture-perfect day."

"Jesse, that's enough," Dad warns.

"Well, someone has to tell her. Look, she's like a deer stuck in headlights."

Layla reaches her hand out and gives my shoulder a gentle squeeze. I notice her silence.

"You don't think I can make Christmas pretty?" I stammer.

"Oh sweetheart, it's not that. It's just...well, I have an aesthetic I need to keep in mind and..."

"So what, you just thought you'd stage a Christmas to present to your followers?"

"Come on, Hol, it's not like anything on social media is real anyway," Layla tries to defuse the situation.

I shrug off her hand. "Are you kidding me?"

"I'm out." Jesse stands.

"Sit back down," Mum growls, "we'll wait for Digby to see if he has everything he needs."

"Come on, Mum. You don't need me. Most of the pictures will be of you with your stuff or closes ups of your stuff. If he doesn't have one good shot with me in it by now then he's not worth the hefty price tag I'm sure you're paying him." Jesse leans over to Mum and gives her a quick kiss on the cheek. "I have to pick up Bridie from some girls wine tour thing soon anyway."

"Should she be drinking in her condition?" Dad asks.

"Relax, Dad. She's not drinking."

"I'm leaving too." I stand.

"No you're not."

"If he can leave, why can't I?"

"I need to go too. Connor and I have a thing...." Layla keeps her answer vague as usual.

Mum rolls her eyes and throws her hands up in the air. "After all the work I put into this..."

"Okay, Jolly family, we're looking good so far," Digby enters the room, waving his camera around.

"Well, they're all leaving," Mum says annoyed.

"Oh," Digby gives her a look that shows he shares her annoyance. "Doesn't matter. You're the star. They can go. Their bit is done."

The three of us make our way out, giving Mum and Dad a kiss. I throw in a little hug for Dad who has to endure God knows how much more of this. My brother, sister and I exit at the same time, letting out a collective groan as the heat hits us, reminding us just how cool we had been for the past couple of hours.

"You good?" Jesse says as he throws his Ray-Bans over his eyes.

"Can you believe her?" I say indignantly.

"Have you even started buying decorations? Have you ordered the turkey? The prawns?" Layla shoots me a doubtful look over the rim of her oversized glasses.

"Yes." *No.*

"Look at it this way Hol, now the pressure is off a little. Mum has her photos so she will be able to enjoy the day, no matter how it looks."

She means for her words to be of comfort, but it came out as an insult. My family's lack of confidence in my decorating skills has really thrown me.

"Peace out, sisters. Catch ya Chrissy Eve."

"You mean my birthday!" I shout after my big brother, but he does nothing to show he hears me or cares as he continues to walk away.

"It's still okay for me to bring Connor, right? I'm so excited for you to finally meet him."

I nod. "Sure. Sure."

"Great. Well listen, shout out if you need a hand with decorating. I helped Mum with her house so..."

"So what, Lays?"

"I'm just *saying* I picked up a few tricks from the stylists if you want help."

"Does anyone in this family have *any* faith in my ability to chuck up a tree and hang some baubles off it?"

Layla simply smiles and waves. "Just shout out, okay? Bye. Love you."

Feeling like a dejected kid who can't be trusted with the glue, I stalk to my car. *I'll show them.* I'll put on the most perfect Jolly Christmas, and then they'll be sorry. I know exactly where I needed to start. Christmas tree, here I come.

Chapter Two

Sunday, 19th December – 6 days to go

"The lady at the other Target said this store definitely has one," I say, scrolling around on my phone as Shawn's car makes the slow crawl towards the shopping centre.

"Did you ask them to hold it for you?" Shawn's patience is wearing thin.

I get it. Mine would too if my best friend pulled me away from the comforts of an air-conditioned house with a pool to drive around the peninsula looking for a Christmas tree six days before Christmas.

I shake my head. "She said they couldn't, which is just ridiculous."

"No, what's ridiculous is you shopping for a Christmas tree a week out from Christmas."

"Six days."

"Oh, excuse me," Shawn mocks.

"And not just any tree, *the* tree. Aaannnd, it might surprise you to know that I did in fact actually try and buy this one back in November, but they had already sold out."

It doesn't surprise him because I have talked nonstop about hosting Christmas since I moved into my place in October, which he helped me to do of course. He's my constant go-to whenever I need help. Moving places? Shawn shows up with a rented truck and matching t-shirts saying "Straight Outta My Parent's Place" in the style of the Straight Outta Compton icon. Photocopier jammed at work? Shawn knows all the right buttons to push to fix the problem. My grade three student throwing up in the classroom bin? Shawn's on it. Okay, that last one was only because we were running a team-teaching activity, and we were in the hall with our two grades. I don't know what I would have done otherwise. Basically, what I'm saying is, Shawn is my knight in shining armour. As handsome as one too. And so completely and utterly off limits.

"Did you try online?" He questions.

"They don't sell this tree online."

"What is the damn thing made of? Gold?"

The corners of my mouth lift. "It's a six-foot tree that is covered in snow. And not the cheap looking spray stuff that wears off the second you put a decoration on it. It's thick stuff that actually looks like real snow."

"But we live in Australia."

"Mm, so?"

"We have three mountains where it snows for about a month every year. Plus, it's *summer*."

"You know, I've never actually seen real snow."

"I'm not surprised since we practically live in a desert. Why are you buying a snow-covered tree anyway? You know, I've never understood the fascination with a white Christmas. I mean, there's a whole bunch of people that live in the Southern Hemisphere where it's summer for Christmas. No snow."

"Snow covered Christmas trees are a trigger for you. I'll file that away."

"I just don't get it. It does not represent our Christmas whatsoever."

"But it's the romance of it."

"Oh geez," he rolls his eyes.

"Besides, Mum has always loved a white Christmas, so I have to have all the things snowy. And that includes the tree."

"The tree we've driven around to four different Target's for?"

"Correct. And when you help me put it up, you will see that it was all worth it."

"Wait – what?"

"Okay, I can't see any car spo..." I mutter.

"Because it's the last weekend before Christmas," he interrupts.

"So, why don't you just circle, and I'll meet you in the taxi bay with the tree?"

"Whatever you say, Mrs Claus."

Shawn pulls into the vacant taxi rank, and I quickly slip out of the car before he tries to merge back in between the cars circling for a spot. No one wants to let him in, and I can see his face turn red as I look over my shoulder at him. He has that pinched look of confusion on his face, the same one he has during staff meetings. I smile to myself ignoring my instincts to think he looks cute and quickly make my way into the shop.

The person greeting the customers at the entrance looks like this shop is the last place they want to be. The woman is maybe Mum's age and has a sour look on her face like all these customers are coming and going to personally inconvenience her. I remember working in retail as a teen, so I empathise with her. She's probably had to deal with some pretty crappy customers. Christmas brings out the worst in shoppers. I hurry past her and get in a "Hello" before she does, thinking I'm making her life a little easier, but it just seems to annoy her even more. I sidestep a wayward toddler and power walk to the Christmas section. The display of trees peek over the top of all the other displays, calling to me like a homing beacon. When I reach the display, there are only a few trees in boxes left. I inspect the shelf for the right one and when I find its white box, I let out a sigh of relief and place my hand on it at the same time someone from the other side pulls it out. I put both my hands on it and pull it back towards me.

"Excuse me," a male voice says from the other side of the display, "I had that first."

Keeping one hand on the box, I gently remove the other and push a Minnie and Mickey Christmas statue to the side so I can see who is trying to steal my Christmas tree. He's tall, dressed in a non-descript white t-shirt and wearing a less than impressed look on his face. He's all sandy hair, sharp edges, strong jawline and piercing blue eyes. My grip must falter slightly, and he pulls the box back in his direction. Despite not being my type, I unashamedly decide to flirt my way out of this. I am not leaving this shop without that tree.

"Excuse me," I smile and do the whole little look down and look back up at him under my fluttering eye lashes thing. I even pull a wayward strand of hair behind my ears. "I believe I had my hand on it first."

"No, you didn't." He snaps.

Okay, so flirting didn't work. Fine. Time to play hardball. "Yes. I did. This is my tree. I had my hand on it first."

"You sound like a spoilt five-year-old." He tugs at the box again.

I place my free hand back onto the box and using as much force as I can muster, I yank the box back to my side.

"And you sound like a rude, arrogant, jerk."

He pulls the box back towards himself, in the process pulling me forward and off balance so my shoulder slams into the top shelf. I let out scream of pain and instinctively grab at my shoulder, letting go of the box and handing the stranger his victory.

"Hey! That was dirty." My brows furrow, and I growl at him.

"You're the crazy lady trying to steal my tree."

I gasp. "*Your* tree? I had my hand on it first!"

He shakes his head. "Whatever. I have it."

"Because you assaulted me!"

"You fell into the display yourself," he states and begins to walk away with the boxed tree.

I grab a Target staff member who just happens to be walking past. "Excuse me, but that man just stole my tree."

The impatient worker looks between me and the man walking away with the white box over his shoulder. I hate to admit that I am impressed he can carry it like that.

"Your tree?" The worker rolls his eyes at me.

"Yes. I had my hand on it first, and he literally yanked it away from me. I fell into the shelf!"

"I don't get paid enough to deal with this shit," the employee says and simply walks away leaving me with my mouth hanging open and treeless.

Shawn pulls in almost the moment I end the call telling him that I am outside. Still rubbing my sore shoulder, I slide into the car and buckle up.

"Is there some sort of magic spell we're supposed to say to make the tree appear?" he mocks.

"I was robbed."

"What do you mean robbed? Like seriously robbed?" He looks concerned.

I indicate for him to pull out into the carpark traffic and tell him about my run-in with The Tree Stealer. He does his best to stifle a laugh. "That's the most Holly story of the day."

"Yeah, well, thanks to that jerk, I no longer have a tree."

"There were none left in the store?"

"Only the crappy snowless little ones."

"Why don't you just get one of those? Your place isn't that big anyway. A six-foot tree would take up your whole lounge room."

I rest my head back against the seat. "You don't get it."

I fiddle with the air vents to make sure the air conditioning hits me in the right way. Shawn is like me and only uses the cooling on the face setting. I don't understand people that have it on the face and feet setting; it's such a waste of cool air. Hit me in the face with all the coolness, my feet will cope. Besides, cold feet are never pleasant. Ever.

"Holly, you know Christmas isn't about the tree...."

"Nope," I hold up a hand to stop the speech he is about to give.

One thing you should know about Shawn is that he is a Good Person. He's always looking for opportunities to learn and grow and encourages other people to do the same. He's far more chilled than I and that is one of the reasons I like being around him so much. He brings a sense of peace to my life. But not right now. Right now, I need him to be superficial and consumer-driven to understand my *need* for this Christmas to be the most perfect of Christmases. Just once, I need to do something that my parents can be proud of. Just once, I need to give Jesse a reason not to belittle me. And just once, I need to show Layla that I can be just as perfect as she is. Just once I need to get something in my life right.

"Shawn, I am normally with you on the whole greater meaning to life thing, but right now, this has to be the opposite of everything we stand for and preach to our students."

In the short twelve months that we have known each other, Shawn has met my parents twice. Once when he came to their house to drop off the first aid kit that I had forgotten to bring home before my first ever excursion with a bunch of eight-years-olds, and a second time when we ran into him down the street at a local cafe. In those two very brief encounters, and probably more due to my endless complaining at work, he has an intricate understanding of what life is like with *Delilah-ful* as a mother.

"So you didn't get a snow-covered tree, why don't you do something different?"

We're stopped behind a line of cars waiting for the lights to change to get out of the shopping centre carpark in the middle of Mornington, which becomes tourist central every summer and reminds us locals how ridiculous having one lane roads are. It just doesn't cope.

"Different?" I roll my head to face him.

His lips broaden into the infamous Shawn Reid smile, the one that reaches to his dark eyes and relaxes anyone in a ten-kilometre radius. He runs a hand over the equally dark stubble on his face.

"Yeah, why not make it more in line with what our actual Christmas is like. Think Australian native flowers and animals."

"You want me to hang a Christmas-hat-wearing-koala ornament from my non-existent tree?"

"If you want to. But that's the point, Hol. It's your place. You can do Christmas however you want and still make it look Instagrammable for *Delilah-ful*."

I give him a suspicious look. "Are you trying to convert me to your non-romancing Christmas ways?"

"An Aussie Christmas can be just as romantic as a snow-covered one." He says and it almost sounds like a promise.

"Tell that to my under-boob sweat."

This time, Shawn lets out a mighty laugh, and I can't help but join in. I like making him laugh. I straighten up and remind myself that I cannot have thoughts like that. Shawn has made it pretty clear that we are just friends. A whole-body cringe takes over as I remember the very reason why I cannot have thoughts like that. I inwardly pull a face as I try and stop my brain from replaying that hideous moment where he moved back from my incoming lips at Gregor's party. *Urgh, stop it.*

"I don't...I don't even have a comeback for that one."

"One point for me," I tease.

He smiles at me, and I swear I see his cheeks colour ever so slightly. He looks down and lets out a nervous laugh. *Too far, Holly.* Way to make this gorgeous man uncomfortable.

"So," I say to recover the awkward silence that has quickly filled the space between us, "an Aussie Christmas, hey?"

He shrugs his shoulders. "Lean into it. Go all out. Just

because *Delilah-ful* has always done it a certain way, doesn't mean you have to."

I think it over for a moment. Actually, that's a complete lie. I get totally lost in his eyes and forget what it is I am supposed to be pretending to think about.

"What do you reckon?" he says, pulling me out of my daydream.

"Yep. Yep. Good. I'm good. Yep. An Aussie Christmas themed Christmas at mine."

"Or just Christmas?" he mocks, and I roll my eyes at him. "You know, we decorate our tree with all different colours."

I gasp, playing along with his joke. "No!"

"Yep. Mum still hangs the Christmas decorations me and my brothers made when we were in kindergarten."

"Stop it."

"She even has a mix of snow-covered trinkets and Australian ones. No coherency. No theme."

"The horror!" I throw a dramatic hand to my brow, and Shawn laughs again.

"We don't even do a turkey on Christmas Day!"

"Wait – what? Seriously?"

He nods. "Yeah, we normally just do a barbie and seafood."

It's foreign to me. My family has always done the traditional roast turkey for Christmas lunch. Sure, like most Australian households, we do prawns and salads because it's too hot for roast vegetables, but there is always a roast turkey front and centre on the Christmas table. I'm not really much of a turkey fan, or of meat in general to be honest, but we've always done it that way.

"What do you normally do after lunch?" I ask, as if Shawn's family Christmas traditions are an exotic experience.

He shrugs. "Hang out by the pool. Go to the beach for a bit of beach cricket. Why, what do you guys do?"

I think about previous Christmas days. What do we do? There seems to be a big emphasis on the morning and the lunch but afterwards.... I guess we don't really do a lot.

"I don't know. We kinda do our own thing. Read. Watch a movie."

"Your parents live across the road from the beach. Don't you go there?"

I shake my head. "They're not really beach people. They just like the look of it."

He shakes his head in return. "That's weird."

"Oh, you think that's weird? Wait 'til I tell you about the photoshoot we just did this morning."

A car honks behind us signalling the light has turned green.

"Can't wait to hear this one. Tell me on the way."

"Where are we going?"

"To get you a tree."

Chapter Three

Sunday, 19th December – 6 days to go

When Shawn said we were going to get me a tree, the last place I expected to find myself was a Christmas Tree Farm. It doesn't sound so ridiculous when I tell you that neither one of us has ever had a real Christmas tree before and therefore know very little about what we are doing. Neither one of us had thought beyond the buying of the Christmas tree; like, how would we get it home? Shawn drives a very sensible Ford Focus. It makes me giggle every time to see him try and fold his tall frame into this little hatchback. It was his mother's car that she gifted to him when he turned eighteen so she could buy herself a brand-new SUV, and Shawn is too much of a "if it ain't broke, don't fix it" kind of guy to buy himself a new car. As he has told me on many occasions, "It gets me from point A to point B". Only today, I doubt very much that it is going to get a real Christmas tree to point B.

We enter the farm a short half an hour before closing time, and there are still a number of people hunting for their perfect tree. I take comfort in the fact that there are other people like me who have left buying a tree until this late in the game.

"See," I whisper to Shawn, pointing around at the couples and families hunting for a tree, "I'm not the only one leaving it late to buy a tree."

"They're hunting for real ones. They get a free pass. Anyone who has a fake tree should be organised and have it up by December first."

"That's very specific."

"Hello there, how can I help you two today?" A sweaty yet cheery lady waddles up to us.

She swats away a fly and holds a small battery-operated fan to her face. She gives Shawn a look as if trying to place him, like he was a familiar face. He gets this a lot.

"Bit hot to be out here all day." Shawn smiles at her, ignoring the puzzled look on her face.

Of course, she smiles back. "Too right, love. Just about melted out here."

"We won't keep you long. We're looking for a Christmas tree."

"Well, you've come to the right place," the woman beams, and Shawn and I appease her by giving a small laugh.

"My friend here," Shawn points to me and the woman raises her eyebrows at him in disbelief, "needs an impressive tree for her first Christmas."

"Nothing too big apparently," I say, and the woman shoots me a look to quieten me down. This conversation is between her and Shawn.

"She lives in a small unit. Maybe something about five foot seven, five foot eight?"

"Shawn! I'm five eight. The tree needs to be taller than me."

"You're five six on a good day, Hol."

The woman chuckles. "Follow me you two. Watch your step. It's a hot day. Seen a coupla snakes today."

"Snakes?" My palms immediately sweat, and my heart beats in my throat.

"Well, what did you expect out here, love? This way."

I turn to Shawn and latch onto his arm, gripping it tight. "I can't go. You go pick one for me."

"Come on, Hol. You'll be right. I'll protect you from any..."

"No, you don't understand. I am petrified of snakes."

"Oh, I know. I was the one who had to take the kids in to the reptile enclosure on the excursion to the zoo."

"Exactly. Shawn, I cannot move. Literally. My feet are planted to the ground."

We look down at my feet. Shawn gives me a little push to see if he can get me off balance. He can't.

"Huh."

"See what I mean! I can't tell if I'm sweating because it's hot or because I'm afraid."

"Holly, you're shaking." I only notice my body is shaking when he mentions it. "You want me to carry you? Piggyback style," he offers in earnest.

As much as I would really like to be that close to him, the thought of my sweaty and sticky body against his, wandering around a tree farm as the sun tries it's best to melt us all, is enough to nip that thought in the bud before it explodes. I shake my head instead.

"You want to wait in the shop?"

Now that I know there has been a snake sighting, I don't want to be anywhere near here. My preference would be waiting at home, far away from the snakes. I shake my head again. He reaches into the pockets of his shorts and pulls out the car keys.

"You want to wait in the car?" I nod and take the keys. "Okay, I won't be long."

"Pick me a nice one."

"Of course." He smiles and walks off towards the lady who is waiting for him a few metres into the farm.

"And make sure there are no snakes hiding in the tree!" I shout after him.

He simply waves at me, and I know he'll do everything in his power to pick the best-looking tree without snakes in it.

. . .

I won't freely admit it, but a six-foot tree would have definitely overwhelmed my small lounge room. It's normally only big enough for a two-seater couch, TV and a couple of floor pillows; now it's home to a small but voluptuous tree whose scent fills up the whole unit.

"And you're sure there are no snakes in it?" I ask for the fifth time.

Shawn is being good about it. He simply smiles at me and begins checking the tree again.

"It's just they can hold on really tight you know, wrap themselves around the tree." I do my best impression of a snake wrapped around a tree and nearly lose my balance.

"I promise you, all we bought home was a tree. No snake. Although it would really add to your Australiana theme."

I throw a pillow at him which he catches while he chuckles. "No snakes, no spiders, no ants, no insects – nothing." Shawn stands, dusting his hands together.

"Thank you."

"Anything for you Miss Jolly," he says in a weird, posh, English accent for no apparent reason, and we give each other a what-was-that look.

"You wanna hang round for pizza? It's the least I can offer for all of the help you've given me today."

Shawn checks his phone, and I check my nerves; calm down ladies. Why am I nervous about his answer? It's a simple "thank you" pizza, no feelings are being confessed. Unless he can see through my offer? I believe this is what people call projecting. I think I got too much sun today.

"I honestly don't mind helping you out, but I'm also not going to turn down a pizza."

"The Lot?" I ask, already knowing his answer.

"Extra anchovies," we say in unison, and I pull a disgusted face.

"You're the only person I know who likes anchovies," I say as I walk away into the kitchen to order two large pizzas.

Shawn makes himself at home as he has done many times in the last two months since I moved in. I don't have a lot, but I like to think it's at least a bit homely. I'm going for the whole boho chic look but right now it's more bare bones and bare walls chic. I have grand plans and numerous Pinterest boards at the ready.

Despite its lack of decor, it feels like home, my home. Initially I was worried about living by myself and thought that perhaps I should rent with my sister or a friend for a while, but it was actually Jesse, of all people, who finally convinced me to take the plunge and buy my own place. Or more accurately, his wife, Bridie, who was far more delicate with her words than he has ever been.

I honestly wonder what a gem like Bridie sees in my brother. Whilst she delicately pointed out all the pros of home ownership, Jesse merely pointed out that no one could ever take me seriously if I was edging closer to thirty and still living at home. Especially not our parents. I guess that was a big enough motivator for me.

I fill up two glasses with wine I had chilled in the fridge but stop short before entering the lounge room when I hear Shawn's whispered voice on the phone to someone.

"Sorry, something's come up. Yeah, I know. Tell the fellas I'll catch 'em next time. Nah mate, all good, all good. See ya later."

My stomach does a flip as I realise Shawn had plans and cancelled them for me. I try my best to hide a smile and not read too much into what I overheard. Maybe I misheard? Maybe he's simply too tired to go out after I made him run around all afternoon in the heat looking for Christmas trees? I suck in a deep breath and try to steady myself. *Just friends, Holly. Just friends.*

Chapter Four

Monday, 20th December – 5 days to go

One of the perks of being a schoolteacher is definitely the school holidays. In particular, the summer holidays. This year by pure chance, we have a week off before Christmas which means I have plenty of time to get my unit Christmas ready. The downside of being a teacher is that it is hard to switch off, even on holidays, and I wake up in a panic at six am thinking I'm late for school. I have never been late to school, not even once as a student and definitely never since I became a teacher; in fact, I usually arrive at least forty-five minutes early each day preparing for my class. The more experienced teachers mock me for having the enthusiasm they have since lost, but the other younger teachers are often there at the same time as me, knocking back a coffee and finishing off some laminating.

Shawn was often one of those early-to-school teachers too. We got into a habit very early on in the year of shouting coffees for each other every morning until Shawn bought in an old Nespresso machine. Then we took it in turns to buy the pods which we kept hidden from the rest of the staff. I think of him now as I cradle a fresh brew in my favourite mug. Shawn was the first friend I made at work this year. He was a friendly experienced face to this inexperienced grad teacher. And I nearly lost it all with that almost kiss. I screw my face up when I think about it and try and think of anything other than that night.

I pick up my phone and scroll through social media. Absent-mindedly, I find my way to the *Delilah-ful* Instagram page and see that Mum has uploaded a new picture. It's one of a sunset with some prophetic words of wisdom underneath. I don't bother reading it because I know it will be something she's taken from Pinterest. She is very careful about what she puts out on social media and even more careful about the words she publishes so as not to offend any one of her nearly six hundred thousand followers. The last thing *Delilah-ful* wants to face is cancel culture and ruin her brand.

I roll my eyes and open the camera app on my phone – barefaced and with a rumpled mess of bed hair, I tilt my head towards the phone and smile with my lips closed. My fingers run over the screen and I post the selfie to my linked social accounts with the caption "Morning" and a peace sign. I don't really know what possess me to do it. It's not really a rebellious act but after living in a carefully curated *Delilah-ful* world, I just want to show something less...perfect, I guess. Not that I have the reach she does. My account is private, and I have less than a hundred followers. My first like comes in followed by a direct message. A smile lights up my face when I see the username: @Reidy_Reid.

@Reidy_Reid: Nice pic.

@Miss_Holly: Thanks *smiley face emoji* what are you doing up this early?

@Reidy_Reid: Couldn't sleep. You?

@Miss_Holly: Same. I kept thinking about the snake.

@Reidy_Reid: Lol! The one at the farm that is definitely not in your tree.

@Miss_Holly: Fears are not rational.

@Reidy_Reid: Do you need me to check it out again? If you're not going to sleep having a real tree in the house then maybe we should get a fake one.

@Miss_Holly: No, it's perfect *love heart emoji* I'll be fine tonight, but maybe you can just check it one more time *snake emoji*

@Reidy_Reid: *Face palm emoji* I'm surprised you didn't ask to check the truck, make sure none hitched a ride over.

@Miss_Holly: *screaming face emoji* should I have done that?

@Miss_Holly: OMG what if one hitched a ride under the truck and is outside my unit just slithering around?!

@Reidy_Reid: Why did I say anything?

@Miss_Holly: Could that happen?

@Miss_Holly: Shawn?

@Miss_Holly: Shawn?

@Miss_Holly: SHHHHAAWWWNNN??!!

@Reidy_Reid: Sorry, just had to get my eggs out. Am I still picking you up at nine?

@Miss_Holly: Of course because I am NOT leaving this house until I know there is no snake slithering around out there.

@Reidy_Reid: You can't see me but just imagine me rolling my eyes.

@Miss_Holly: There's an emoji for that.

@Reidy_Reid: See you at nine.

@Miss_Holly: Wait, you never answered my question. Shawn?

@Miss_Holly: Shawn?

@Miss_Holly: SHAWN???!!!!

Chapter Five

Monday, 20th December – 5 days to go

Finding Australiana Christmas decorations is a lot harder than I thought it would be. Almost all decorations the shops stock are standard snow-covered everything: snowmen, snow covered trees, people dressed in beanies and scarfs, or mice. I'm not sure I understand the obsession with mice and Christmas, but if they show up at my place, they'll be quickly shown the door. We settle on a kangaroo in sunglasses and a Santa hat, a koala in sunglasses and a Santa hat, and a Santa dressed in– yep, you guessed it– sunglasses and a Santa hat. Although he is also wearing a Hawaiian shirt, board shorts and holding a surfboard. I also pick up an armful of gold and red baubles and a string of fairy lights.

"Don't let me forget. I have a bag in the boot for you," Shawn says as he turns into the supermarket carpark.

"Well, don't leave me hanging in suspense."

He chuckles. "It's not that exciting. I picked up some pine cones on my morning run. Thought you could use them as decorations. I chucked in the leftover spray paint from craft day too."

"You want me to spray paint pine cones like our grade three

students and display them where exactly? My mother has never once hung any decoration we ever made as children. I don't think she'll be too thrilled to see my attempt at grade three craft on the Christmas table."

"Shhh." Shawn holds a finger up to his lips. "Remember, we're not doing what *Delilah-ful* wants, we're doing what Holly wants."

"Sounds more like what Shawn wants. You're the crafty one."

"Good point," he says and swings the car into one of the very few spots left.

There is an unspoken rivalry among primary school teachers about who has the best decorated, themed classroom. I knew this was a thing before I even started my job because on my teaching rounds, one of my supervisors took great pride in showing off her jungle-themed room that had matching name tags, tub labels, class lists – everything. It will come as a shock to absolutely no one who knows me, but I do not have a crafty bone in my body. I lack the patience for it, or so I've been told. This year my room was next to Shawn's. Shawn decorated his classroom by season which meant that he changed everything about the way his room looked four times this year. I could barely manage once. Nothing in my room matches. There are no fancy displays or clever cut-outs of the kids' faces on paper flowers to celebrate spring; no, my room is a chaotic mess of alphabet charts, times tables, vocab words and student work plastered wherever I could stick it. Next year I promise to up my game.

"The golden goose is a fresh turkey," Shawn says, turning to me as we enter the shop like he is explaining a match-winning game plan. "If they have none left, which is highly likely as we are a week out from Christmas," he reminds me like a child who's been told *so many times*, "then you'll want to get a frozen one. It's usually just the breast, but it'll be just as good."

I nod. "And if they don't have either?"

"Then we're stuffed."

"Impeccable pep talk."

"It's why you bring me along. Excuse me," Shawn adds as he taps the shoulder of an employee who turns around to greet him with wide eyes. We both know what is coming next.

"Whoa, dude, you look like that dude from *The Matrix*."

"Keanu Reeves," Shawn and I say in unison.

He's young Keanu in the face, but old Keanu with the long hair and beard. This happens at least once every time we go out, usually they place him as a Keanu look alike, or they stare at him puzzled, trying to place him like the lady at the tree farm. We try to ignore it because Shawn hates it, but he doesn't let it show. He simply offers a smile and continues with the conversation.

"We're looking for fresh turkeys. Can you point us in the right direction?"

The employee eyes him suspiciously as if still trying to figure out if the real-life Keanu Reeves is standing in front of him. I take a quick glance at the features that are so familiar to me, and I decide it's the long hair and Shawn's preference for dressing in black that make him so Keanu-like. And the eyes. His face is still young though. I tilt my head and take him in.

"Stop it." He whispers to me as the employee points us in the right direction.

We thank him and make our way over to the fridges.

"You know, it's not a bad thing to be told you look like Keanu Reeves."

"Why? Why is it never Han Solo?" he asks a little more dramatically than I was expecting.

"Your *Star Wars* obsession is alarming if you want to look like a hundred-year-old Harrison Ford."

"Actually, I'd prefer young Harrison Ford from the original and the best movies in the whole series."

"Well, everyone loves Keanu Reeves. He's a global treasure. He's like the nicest guy on the planet and super-hot."

"Really?" Shawn raises his eyebrows, and I feel my cheeks flush. "He's also old enough to be your dad Miss Harrison-Ford-Objector."

"Why do you have to ruin it?"

"You also forgot to say he's a total badass."

"Absolutely he is. Now come on John Wick and let's get me a turkey."

As we make our way to the fresh turkey section, which from a distance is looking bare, I stop short.

"Oh. My. God!" I shout louder than necessary and grab at Shawn's bare arm. "It's that guy again, the one that stole my Christmas tree."

"Which one?"

"The only guy in the fridge section!" I say impatiently.

"That guy? That chiselled jawed, bright blue-eyed guy that looks like..."

"Every guy in every Hallmark movie ever, yes. Do you want me to get his number for you?" I say sarcastically.

"See, why can't I look like him?"

I ignore Shawn and tap The Tree Stealer on the shoulder. He spins around, turkey in his arms. Crap.

"Hey! Remember me?"

The blue-eyed Christmas Tree Stealer stares at me blankly.

"You stole my Christmas tree!" I say rather loudly drawing a few curious glances from passing customers.

"Oh, *you*."

"Yes, *me*! It's not fair that you stole the last Christmas tree and now you have," I glance around his shoulders to the fridge, "the last turkey."

"I don't believe I took the last Christmas tree in all of existence."

Shawn strikes a martial arts pose and waves his fingers for The Tree Stealer to come closer.

"Hand over the turkey," he whispers.

My eyes widen. "What are you doing?"

"I've seen *The Matrix*. I know how this goes."

"Oh yeah, right, you do look like that guy from those movies," the Christmas Tree Stealer concedes.

32

"Whatever," I throw my hands up, "just give me the turkey. Fair's fair."

"Except, I got it first. So, I'm gonna go. With the turkey." A smug smile dances across his face as he gives Shawn and I a short wave.

"That's not fair!" I shout to his back as he walks away. "You ruined Christmas. You're The Christmas Ruiner! I hope Santa brings you a lump of coal."

A portly man dressed in tie dye walks past our turkey stealing scene and mutters something under his breath about the needless slaughter of turkeys for human festivities.

"Right on," Shawn says, and I give him an unimpressed look. "What? It sounds like something Keanu would say."

I roll my eyes. "Come on, let's go get a stupid frozen one."

Chapter Six

Tuesday, 21st December – 4 days to go

Mondays are fabulous when you don't have to work but Tuesdays are even better! Yesterday was the first official day of school holidays and I've never loved a Monday more; mainly because I knew it would be followed by other days off unlike a public holiday – those Mondays off are just a tease.

I vowed this morning that I am definitely going to forget about The Christmas Ruiner and get on with my holidays and celebrations. I arrive at the shops to do some last-minute Christmas shopping for the family, including one very special present for Mum and Dad which requires me meeting up with my siblings. Whilst both Layla and Jesse are still working right up until Christmas Eve, they've agreed to meet me at Southland Shopping Centre on their lunch breaks for this one particular present. That's where I am now as I wait for them outside the Myer department store dressed in the ugliest, most over-the-top Christmas jumper on a piping hot day. At least the centre is air-conditioned. I managed to find a website that sold purposefully ugly Christmas jumpers and bought three matching ones. Think red, green and white knits covered in many bells, tinsel and gold trimmings. There are even some fun 3D presents that stick out. They are hideously amazing. A few people smirk at me as I wait for my siblings to arrive. More people try their best to avert their gaze so as not to give offensive looks. Both Jesse and Layla are running late, so I scroll through my phone and send them a message in our group chat.

Rivals Group Chat
11:45am Tues 21st Dec

H: Are you even close to being here?

L: Connor is just dropping me off. We're at the lights on Nepean hwy. Be about five mins

H: Is Connor coming in? I am not prepared to meet your new bf dressed like this.

L: He was going to but there are no car spots. He will probs just drive around until after the pic.

H: So the first time we meet him is with Mum and Dad on my bday?

L: Can't help bad timing.

H: I feel like you could have made it work if you really wanted us to meet him.

L: Relax, Hol. We have forever.

J: Pass me a bucket! I agree with Holly.

H: Are you here, Jesse?

J: Coming up the escalator now.

H: Oh I see you! See you soon Lays.

Jesse comes dressed in suit and tie, and I almost feel bad for him having to wear an outfit like that during summer. But then I remember how much money he earns from that suit, and the feeling disappears.

"That car park is a bloody nightmare." He nods his head as a greeting.

I pull his jumper out of the bag and wave it in his face.

"These are worse than you described." He holds it up, examining it with a sour look on his face.

"Pop it on and see if it fits."

He shakes his head. "Not a chance. I am putting it on two seconds before the photo and removing it immediately after."

"Sorry it's not a designer label," I mock.

I know that this Jesse, the one that looks like he's just stepped off a Tom Ford shoot, is very different to the off-duty Jesse. He really doesn't care for such things outside of the office, but he plays the game well.

"Why are *you* wearing it?"

I shrug my shoulders. "Because it's *fun*? And I spent nearly two hundred dollars getting these babies made and shipped to us before Christmas, so I intend to get my money's worth."

"I will pay you to take it off."

"Are you embarrassed to be seen with me big brother?" I tease and latch onto him, taking great joy in making him squirm.

He tries to peel me off just as Layla joins us.

"What are you two doing? Why are you wearing that?"

Layla is the opposite of Jesse and me, and more like our mother. She is all about designer labels and looking like she'd stepped off the front cover of *Vogue* every second of her life. I am exhausted by her. As predicted, she immediately screws up her face when I present her with the jumper. She holds onto it by the barest of threads.

"Let's just get this over with. And no putting this picture up online," she warns me. "It's bad enough the people taking the photo have to see me in this jumper."

"Yes, God forbid anyone sees you looking anything but perfect, Layla." I roll my eyes.

There's a lot to be said for sibling rivalry, especially between sisters, but not between Layla and me. I am more than happy to stay in my lane and allow her the attention she craves. Truth be told, she could make a potato sack look like the latest trend.

We ride the escalators to the top floor where we line up for our photo with Santa. Yes, my brilliant Christmas present to our parents is a recreation photo of one from when we were little. I know Dad will get a huge kick out of it. It's difficult to predict how Mum will respond. I remind myself to pick up some of her favourite perfume on the way out as a backup.

"This is humiliating," Jesse says through gritted teeth, "we are the oldest people here without kids."

"Hush you. Next Christmas, this will be you," I whisper shout at him.

"Next Christmas I will have a reason to be here."

"You have a reason now! There's no age limit on Santa photos you know."

"There are things called unwritten social rules, and I'm pretty sure this is one of them."

"I really hope you lean into your inner child when my niece or nephew gets here. Poor Bridie."

Jesse scratches at his forehead, subtly giving me the finger as he does so.

"Okay, who is next?" The perky woman dressed as an elf turns around to face us.

"That would be us. We had a booking for Jolly," I say with a smile.

She takes in my jumper. "Love the Christmas spirit! Ah yes, here you are. Jolly for three. Come right this way."

Santa chuckles as we step forward towards him. The set-up is a little different to the original picture we are going off, but the vibe remains the same: blues, silvers and snow-covered props. I smile to myself and think about what Shawn would say if he were here.

"Ho! Ho! Ho! Have we been naughty or nice?" Santa plays his part as children stare, wide-eyed with glee that three grown adults are going to have their picture taken with Santa.

"Well, *I* have definitely been good. I'm not sure about these two though," I joke.

"Ho! Ho! They certainly don't have the same cheery disposition as you do young lady. Perhaps they are on the naughty list."

"I'm on the can-we-hurry-up-and-get-this-done-I-have-to-get-back-to-work-list," Jesse grumbles as he pulls the jumper over his head. It fits him snugly and I catch the perky elf giving him a second glance. *Gross.*

"Ho! Ho! Where has your Christmas spirit gone, young man?"

"Maybe you can bring him some this year," I muse.

Jesse gives me the side-eye glare, and Santa chuckles at our exchange.

"Hi...um, Santa?" Layla speaks with uncertainty, "we just want to recreate a photo from our childhood for our parents. Would that be okay? Hol, show him the photo."

I hold out my phone to him.

"Shawn is calling you," Santa says.

"What?" I drag the phone back and see a photo of Shawn pulling a ridiculous face appear on the screen. He tagged the photo to his contact ages ago, and yet it still makes me laugh every time I see it. I try to cover a smile as I bury my head to reject the call, reminding myself to call him after this. I pull up the photo from our childhood and show it to Santa.

He chuckles. "Ho! This shall be a fun one."

We each take a look at the picture, not that we need too. It's been sitting on the kitchen hutch, framed, since we took it. It is the one picture Mum and Dad refuse to take down, so we try in earnest to recreate it perfectly. Of course, when we were little, Mum dressed us in matching tartan outfits, and since Jesse flat out refused to recreate that element of the photo, we compromised and got ugly jumpers instead.

Layla takes her place first next to Santa and sits up straight, arranging her jumper so all the ugliness can be seen. She pretends to clap her hands and slaps a big, cheesy grin across her face. I sit on the arm of the chair and fold my arms across my chest getting ready to pull an exaggerated grumpy face, and Jesse reluctantly sits on top of Santa's knee, with one arm around his neck and the other flung open. One leg is firmly on the ground now that he is tall enough and another is sprung up in the air. He pulls a ridiculously happy face, and the photographer takes the picture. As soon as the camera clicks, Jesse jumps off Santa's lap and pulls his jumper off.

"Wait!" I shout. "Should we do another just in case it didn't work?"

"I'm sure it did," Jesse states, already jumper-free. He looks to the person behind the laptop and they give a thumbs up. "Thank God." Jesse stalks away and leaves Layla and me to thank the whole Santa team.

Another person dressed as an elf instructs me to wait next to the laptop for our print out. As I ordered the package online, there's very little paperwork to fill in.

"Right, I'm off." Jesse looks at his watch.

"Don't you want to see the picture?" Layla asks.

"Not particularly. I'll see it on Christmas Day when you give it to Mum and Dad." He throws the jumper at me.

"Bye." I say annoyed as he walks away, not even looking back. "Why is he always such a dick?"

"He's not normally that bad. I guess he's pretty stressed out with work and with the baby coming," Layla offers.

She has a very different relationship with Jesse than I do. I was the one that came along and ruined his only-child status and took the focus away from him when he was two. Layla was the one who took the focus away from me, and, at four years of age, that pleased his tiny mind, like some sort of revenge had been dealt.

"So who's Shawn anyway?" Layla asks and drags me out of my childhood memories.

"Huh?"

"When you first showed Santa your phone, he said Shawn was calling you."

"Oh, just a friend from work." I wave my hand dismissively.

Layla gives me a look that tells me she doesn't believe me. "Mmm hmmm, one that makes you flustered and red?"

"I was not flustered!"

"You are now," she laughs.

Layla and I are not the type of sisters who share intimate details of our lives. We never have. Layla has always been one to do her own thing. I guess we all have when I think about it. Mum and Dad too. They never really fostered family time when we were growing up. Only on special holidays, were we expected to come together and be together as one. The rest of the time we were pretty much left to do our own thing.

"Why was he calling you? You guys have finished work for the year."

"So, we're not allowed to talk outside of work?"

"Is he single?"

I respond to her question by rolling my eyes. Since she has been with Connor, Layla has been on my back about dating and meeting someone. She's one of those people who when they're in a relationship, wants everyone else to be in one too. And when she's not, she wants everyone else to be single too.

"Is he available? You should ask him to Christmas Eve dinner."

"No."

"Why not?"

"Because we're friends."

"Do you not see your friends on your birthday?"

"I'm not going into this with you."

"Oh come on, Holly! You're almost twenty-six. Don't you think it's time to start settling down?"

I fold my arms across my chest. "Did Mum put you up to this?"

She smiles sweetly, which I know means yes. "I just think, personally, that you're leaving it a bit late."

"For what exactly?"

"To get married! Have kids!"

"I'm turning twenty-six not fifty-six! And I don't need life advice from my baby sister."

She sighs. "Just think about it."

I shake my head and try my best not to lose it at my sister in front of all the children lining up for their Santa photo. How dare she insinuate that she knows what I want or what is best for me and my life! She is the worst kind of obnoxious, coupled up...

"Here you are!" The elf says, handing me our picture.

I pull it out of the packaging, and it brings a smile to my face. "It's perfect." I mumble to myself.

"Urgh. I look ridiculous." Layla pulls it closer to her.

I snatch it back like a child. "Well I think Mum and Dad will love it."

She pulls off her jumper and hands it to me. "I'm sure they will. I better get going. Connor is probably sick and tired of circling the carpark. See you Friday night."

She blows me a kiss and gives a little wave, and I hate-stare her down as she walks away. I know that for the rest of the day I will be stewing on our little chat while she's probably already forgotten about it, and that makes me even more angry with her.

"Don't forget to call Shawn back!" she calls out over her shoulder, and I pull a face, mimicking her like the child that I am.

The shopping centre is a hive of activity, and I let myself get lost among the chaos to forget about my sister and her nosy opinions. I have dated *plenty* of men. Okay, well, not plenty, plenty, but I have been out on a few dates and none of them have really been anything special. None of them have really been...Shawn. Try as I might, I can't let go of these feelings I have for him. And I know that he doesn't feel the same way but dating anyone else right now while I have these feelings for him isn't worth it. I'll just work through it, get over him, and then I'll be able to move on. Until then, I'm content. I pull out my phone to call him back when I decide that a message would be better. I only call people in times of emergency.

H: Hey, sorry I missed your call before. Was getting my photo taken with Santa.
　　S: And other things I never thought I'd hear you say. Proof please.

I take a simple picture of the photograph and send it to Shawn. He replies immediately.

S: *crying face emoji* this is my favourite thing ever.
　　H: I know, right? So what's up?

The message bubbles appear and disappear three times and I begin to get nervous about what he is going to say next.

S: I know you're busy with your family on Friday but my brother's band is playing at the local pub. Just wondering if you want to come along and I can shout you a drink for your bday?

I stare at my phone with a goofy grin on my face. I have failed miserably in not letting my imagination run wild. In mere seconds we're engaged, married and have two kids. I let my fantasy life flash before my eyes. It's a very accessible daydream, one I have visited too many times to admit. I remind myself that I have seen his brother's band play before so it's no big deal to be invited to see them again. Only last time, we'd gone with a group of teachers from school. Were they invited this time too? Would Shawn's family be there? Despite how close we are, I haven't met the rest of the Reid family and my stomach turns in knots at the thought of it. Yet I can't help but hope this time will be different. I also read way too much into the fact that he has refused to call the day Christmas Eve and allowed me to have my day as my day.

H: I'd love to! Shoot me through the details.

Chapter Seven

Wednesday, 22ⁿᵈ December – 3 days to go

Delilah-ful is not the type of person you say no to, so when she showed up on my door step unexpectedly this morning to take me shopping, all other plans had to be put on hold. Not that I had any other fascinating plans, but I was going to use the day to wrap the presents I had bought the day before.

"Oh, darling, it is like an oven in here. Why don't you put the air conditioning on?" Mum says distractedly as she glides around my unit.

I'm not exactly sure what she is looking for, but I guess she doesn't find it because she's facing me with her fake smile.

"It is on." I wipe a bead of sweat from my forehead.

"Hmmm, we can still move Christmas Day to...:

"Nope," I hold up my hand, "I'm prepared to have it here. Look at my tree!"

She does, and I can tell she is not impressed. "We've never had a real tree before. The smell is a bit overbearing in this small space, isn't it?"

I know this move, it's the old I'll-plant-the-seed-of-doubt-so-she'll-crumble-and-say-I-can-host-instead move. This time though, I'm not falling for her tricks. I'm going to host the most magnificent Christmas this family has ever had.

"Are those...are those koalas on your tree?"

"Yes, Mum, I thought it might be fun to embrace a typical Aussie Christmas."

She grimaces. "I see."

"I mean, you do the white Christmas so well," I apply the adoration on thick to stroke her ego, "and I thought, instead of trying to match you, which *of course* is no easy feat, I would try something different."

"It sure is different."

I smile as though she gave me a compliment, and we both stand in awkward, sweaty silence. I really hope the cool change comes in and gives my place a chance to cool down and air out, so the day is comfortable.

"So, where exactly are we going?" I ask, and Mum transforms into an excited child. It's frightening.

"You'll see," she grins and wags her finger at me to follow her out the door.

Santa's Place has been a local establishment in our area forever, and it will surprise no one that they know my mother by name. Although they've moved from the large corner property into a much smaller warehouse in the industrial area, they've certainly packed as much Christmas cheer into every conceivable corner of the place. As soon as you walk in your senses are assaulted with a caramel like scent, as well as colour-coded sections of all sorts of Christmas paraphernalia overflowing on the shelves and even hanging from the roof. There is no space that has been left unused. It really is like a Christmas wonderland in here. I remember going to their larger farm all throughout my childhood but haven't step foot in here since I became an adult. Now that I'm here, I wonder why I stopped coming. If this place didn't get you in the mood for Christmas, then nothing would.

"Now I know you have your own thing going on, but I just thought perhaps you might see something you like in here for your place this Christmas," Mum says as we wander through the front of the store into the first open, colour-coded section.

We walk under a perfectly decorated arch, and I immediately want to buy everything. "Mum, this stuff is way out of my budget. It's beautiful, but..."

"Uh ah," Mum wags her finger at me, "my gift to you. Think of it as an early birthday present." She smiles, and I can't help but roll my eyes.

I've lost count of the amount of Christmas-themed birthday presents I have received over the years and none of them were ever really for me. They've been for display on the shelves in the family home but by saying they're a birthday present for me, it helps to justify the cost of another over-priced and unnecessary Christmas trinket. Worse than getting a Christmas-themed present for my birthday is when someone gives me a present and says that it's for my birthday and Christmas. I'm not a shallow or materialistic person, and it's not necessarily the gift that annoys me but the thought behind it, like that you cannot separate my birthday and Christmas, like I'm not worth celebrating in my own right. Everyone else gets to have their birthdays to themselves, why can't I?

I wander the shop and see lots of nice stuff. My immediate default is to find something winter-themed and to be honest, there is a lot of it. I walk upstairs and have a little giggle to myself as I am greeted by life-size kangaroos in Santa hats attached to a sleigh, taking the place of the reindeer. A life-size statue of Santa in a Hawaiian shirt and shorts stands next to the sleigh. I snap a quick picture of it and send it to Shawn.

H: Too much?

S: This is perfect! If you don't get it, I am.

H: *laughing crying emoji* Where would you even put it? Or store it?

S: Details, details! It's amazing.

H: I know you're joking, but I also wouldn't be surprised if you did come down and buy it.

I smile. I really wouldn't put it past Shawn to buy this monstrosity of Christmas.

"Who are you smiling at?" Mum catches me off guard. I had no idea she had come up stairs let alone was standing next to me.

"Huh? What?"

Fumbling to put my phone away like a teenager caught texting their crush was not really helping my case of appearing cool, calm and collected. Mum wags her eyebrows at me, and I ready myself for what is about to come.

"What's his name?"

"What makes you think..."

"Oh Holly, please. I am your mother, and I know that face when I see it. It is the same face you pulled when Craig Watson asked you to the year ten formal."

I pull a face. Craig Watson was a huge mistake. As I try to push that unwanted memory from my brain, she bombards me with questions.

"Is it serious? It's about time you found someone who made you smile like that again. Honestly, Hol, your father and I were starting to worry about you, especially as your brother and sister have settled down. Do you want to invite your special friend to Christmas Eve dinner?"

I poke my tongue out like a child when she says special friend. Is there any worse way to describe someone? It sounds ten kinds of dirty and inappropriate. I put my hand up to stop her from going any further.

"Number one, I am choosing to ignore your little dig at my private life. I am happy, and that's all you need to be worried about," I tell a half truth, "and number two, I was just messaging a friend from work. Emphasis on the *friend* part."

She folds her arms over her chest and surveys me. Her eyes run over me as if deciding whether or not to push the conversation further. Even if she decides to give up, I know this will not be the last time she says her two cents worth about my dating life. I'm a constant disappointment to my mother – I'm single, came to my career late and have only just managed to buy my first home, all things my brother and sister managed to do before me. To her, my home is not a home. It's a unit, and there is a clear distinction in her mind. That's why this Christmas has to go perfectly, to show her that I am more than capable of adulting and doing something other than disappointing her for a change.

"Well, there's no need to get so defensive, Hol. But just so you know, there will be plenty of food if you do change your mind and want to bring someone home on Friday."

"Not changing my mind."

Nope. No way. No how, would I ever bring anyone home to meet the family unless I knew they were The One. I guess that's why we haven't met Layla's boyfriend Connor yet. I don't blame her really. Mum will have them picking out wedding venues and celebrants by the end of the night. That's why Craig Watson was a mistake; poor Craig thought he was arriving to pick up a sixteen-year-old girl for a school dance not meeting his future in-laws and having to decide on the names of his future children.

Mum had told him that my blue eyes mixed with his darker complexion would make for the most beautiful babies. She wasn't even doing it to scare off him off; she was deadly serious. She's been planning her children's weddings since we were born. No wonder Craig dumped me as soon as we made it to the school hall. I haven't brought anyone home since. As far as my family know, I've been living like a nun.

. . .

The first thing I do is pull a cold can of Coke out of the fridge and take it to my final resting place for the evening on my couch, in front of the TV and under the air conditioning duct. All in all, I survived two hours with *Delilah-ful*. She walked out of the Santa shop with bags full of more snow-covered decorations whilst I managed to pick up a table runner. I paid for it myself before she could gift it to me as an early birthday present. Although it's still light out, I've put my Christmas tree lights on and stare at them more than whatever is on the TV. There is something truly magical about twinkling fairy lights when paired with a tree. I look to the presents, finally neatly wrapped under the tree and give myself a little pat on the back. I may just pull this off. My phone buzzes shortly after, and I answer when I see Shawn's name scrawled across the screen.

"I need help. Is it socially acceptable to give my brothers and their partners a combined present to enjoy as a couple or should I buy individual presents? Because my brother-in-law is impossible to buy for."

"I always thought it was easier for guys to buy other guys presents because you kinda know what you like."

"Only if that person has a hobby. Outside of my brother and the twins, Trevor has nothing."

I bring my feet up underneath me. "Are you doing your Christmas shopping now?"

"Yes."

"And you had the audacity to have a go at me for leaving things 'til the last minute!" I shout jokingly down the phone.

"Hey, this is early for me. Normally I shop on Christmas Eve, but I saw the weather forecast and made an executive decision to sit by Mum and Dad's pool all day on the twenty-fourth."

"Don't tell me it's getting hotter."

"Forty-one degrees."

"That's too hot to be in the pool. You'll burn."

"Part of it is shaded. This is all irrelevant. Help me be socially acceptable please."

"I think a combined present is fine. Especially if it's like tickets to something, and you offer to babysit."

"Good call. I knew I kept you around for a reason."

"You mean my beauty isn't enough? You keep me around for my brains as well?"

"Seems new age, doesn't it?"

We share a laugh, and I try not to think about how easy things are with Shawn. Our friendship has always blurred the lines of flirtatious friends and significant other, and that is why I find it so easy to let my imagination run wild and imagine something more with him.

"I still can't believe you're only doing your shopping now."

"Like I said, I usually go on Christmas Eve. If they don't have what I want, then it wasn't meant to be. Besides, I have a really small family to shop for; Mum, Dad, my two brothers, my sister-in-law, my brother-in-law, two nephews and two nieces."

"That still sounds like a lot."

"It's not. Oh, and by the way, we're still on for tomorrow night, right? The lights?"

I smack my hand against my head. I had completely forgotten that I had agreed to go see the Christmas light with Shawn. We had arranged it, well, he had arranged it, before we left school for the end of year break. To be honest, he could ask me to go with him to the opening of an envelope and I'd happily oblige.

Our conversation is interrupted by a loud buzzing sound.

"What is that?" Shawn asks, concerned on the other end of the phone.

I stare up at my ceiling from where the noise came. A blast of hot air escapes the vent I am sitting under and then another loud noise, like a bang, follows and then suddenly, there is no more air from the vents.

"Oh no."

"That doesn't sound good, Holly."

"I think my air conditioner just crapped itself."

My stomach drops as I bring the palm of my hand to my face. Could this get any worse?

Chapter Eight

Thursday, 23rd December – 2 days to go

The alarm softly sings to life next to me. It does not rouse me from my slumber like some kind of graceful princess because I am yet to find this elusive sleep of which people talk. My night consisted of tossing and turning in sweat-sticky sheets, listening to the small portable fan creak as its head turned about the room and swatting away the buzzing fly who favoured the spot just above my left ear. As I stared at the ceiling reliving everything that has ever gone wrong in my entire life, I came to the conclusion that the universe hates me. Or that Murphy was making me his personal subject to prove his theory right.

I peel myself off the sheets and head straight for the shower. Warm water runs from the cold tap and I get very little reprieve from the heat. The only blessing is that Shawn managed to find an aircon guy to come out this morning. We're two days away from the big day, and Shawn has provided a Christmas miracle. At least now I don't feel so awkward about getting him a gift to say thank you for all his help in organising this crap fest of a Christmas.

The aircon guy is coming over before most people are up. Who would have thought that summer was a busy time of year for aircon guys? I mean, besides everyone. You'd think they'd hire more people for this time of year. The knock at my door before seven am is a welcomed sound. I throw on an oversized shift dress, tie a clip in my wet hair and hope that the circles under my eyes are lighter than my mood.

I open the door, my face automatically screws itself up before my sleep-deprived brain can figure out why The Christmas Ruiner is standing at my front door. At least he looks as confused as me.

"Hmm," he says with a puzzled look on his face.

"This cannot be happening," I sigh.

"Only if you want your aircon fixed."

My brain works a little slower when it runs off no sleep and anger, so I actually contemplate sending The Christmas Ruiner home and cancelling Christmas altogether.

"You owe me one, so why not." I open the door wide and gesture for him to come in.

"Owe you one?"

"You stole my tree and my turkey, Mr Christmas Ruiner. The least you can do is fix my aircon."

He nods towards the Christmas tree in the corner. "Looks like you faired okay."

"No thanks to you."

"Right, where's the man hole?"

I take him into the laundry and watch him disappear into the roof. I head back to the kitchen and start the kettle, wondering if I should offer him a cup of something. My need to please people takes over, and I hear myself offering to make The Christmas Ruiner a coffee. He declines, and I'm not sure if I am offended or mad at myself that I bothered to ask in the first place. I think today is one of those days where everything is just going to set me off.

When the coffee finally hits my veins, I feel alive. I can feel its warmth coursing through my body as I start to relax ever so slightly. I hear The Christmas Ruiner's feet land with a thud in the laundry and within seconds he is standing in front of me dusting off his jeans. Who wears jeans in weather like this anyway?

"I've got good news and bad news."

"Of course you do."

"Bad news is, it's definitely broken which is not ideal at the moment. Good news is that it's fixable. Bad news is that I'll need to order in some parts, and they won't come until the new year."

I spray coffee from my mouth. I know, I'm so graceful. "What?!"

"It's an older model so the parts are harder to source. Plus, everyone has pretty much shut down already for the Christmas period."

A lump rises in my throat, and my eyes begin to sting. I swallow hard. I will not cry in front of this man. "Are you sure? What if you just replace the whole thing?"

He chuckles, and I want to slap him. "You'd be up for a fair chunk of change."

"How much?" I bargain like I have a spare chunk of anything lying around.

"Upwards of eight grand, closer to ten." I try not to choke on air as he continues, "And even if you wanted to do that, I still couldn't do anything until the new year anyway. We'd have to order in the unit…"

"Hold up," I interrupt, "essentially, you're telling me, there is nothing you can do."

"Correct."

"Is this a joke? Are you joking?"

"Look, you can try and ring around."

"I have. And so has my friend. You were the only one who could come out this side of Christmas!"

"What can I say? It's a busy time of year. You just got unlucky with the timing. I mean, this heatwave hasn't helped things. Lots of people having trouble."

I eye him suspiciously. "Is this just like another Christmas tree *slash* turkey thing? Like, can you really not help me, or is it that you really don't want to?"

He rolls his eyes. "What was it that you called me? Mr Christmas Ruiner?"

"I guess you're really living up to that moniker."

"I guess so. Look, I can't do anything else here today, but I can order the parts and come back and fit them when they come in. Do you want me to go ahead and do that?"

That would mean I would have to see this arrogant jerk again. I had no other choice. All the other places I rang couldn't even come out to see me, let alone order parts and potentially fix it in a few days' time.

"Whatever," I mumble.

He gets out his phone and makes a few notes before turning to me with a smug smile on his face.

"Have a good Chrissy. Might I suggest heading off to Bunnings and grabbing a couple of free-standing fans. If you can find some."

"Maybe I'll see you there as you poach the last one."

His grin widens as he gives a little wave and heads out the front door. I slump down in front of the cupboards and finally allow the tears to roll down my cheeks. It doesn't take long before the ridiculousness of my week has me both laughing and crying at the same time, making a strange sound that even wild animals would be afraid of. Surely, it couldn't get much worse than this.

Chapter Nine

Thursday, 23rd December – 2 days to go

The day is a complete bust. I drive to three different Bunnings stores across three different suburbs and manage to only snag two free-standing fans. Maybe if the seven of us stand really still on Christmas day, it will be enough. I assemble them and proceed to spend the afternoon sitting in front of both of them on the couch pretending I'm on a boat sailing the high seas, wind in my hair, cool breeze on my face. It cools me down enough, but I still feel sticky, so I shower again and look in the fridge for leftovers for dinner. I'm never really hungry in this kind of weather which is a good thing because I also never really want to cook anything in this type of weather.

Shawn knocks on my door just after eight thirty at night and lets himself in. "Aren't you a sight for sore eyes?" he says as he comes face to face with me and my fans.

"I'm pretending to be Beyonce."

Shawn breaks out into a few dance moves from "All The Single Ladies" and makes me laugh. "I take it the aircon guy didn't work out?"

I gasp, completely forgetting that I hadn't told Shawn about my encounter this morning. "You will never guess who showed up at my door!"

"The air con guy," Shawn says slowly.

"The Christmas Ruiner! He was the air con guy."

"Of all the people..."

"Right? That's what I thought! Apparently, he can't fix it before Christmas, so I spent the day running around trying to find fans."

"That's really rotten luck, Hol. I'm sorry."

"Then why do you have a smile on your face?"

Shawn gives in to the small laugh he is trying to conceal. "So far, this has been the most Holly thing ever."

"You mean because I'm a screw up, and everything I do screws up, and my life is one giant screw ball of a screw up!"

"That's a bit dramatic. Come on, Miss Diva, let's go. I have the night mapped out from the app."

He reaches for my hand which I gladly give him so he can help peel me off the couch. The leather squelches behind me, and I don't bother explaining or excusing myself.

When Shawn said he had the night planned, he was not kidding. I learn that he is very serious about going out and seeing the Christmas lights that people cover their houses in. Normally, my family wanders around our neighbourhood in the hope of stumbling upon something, but not Shawn; he has everything down to a fine art. I didn't even know there was an app for Christmas lights! The first lot we see are cute; lots of hanging blue lights that looks like icicles mixed with kangaroos and deers made out of lights. Someone even has a light giraffe on their front lawn. I enjoy the blow-up Santas with sleighs and the houses with Christmas trees in their front windows.

But those first houses are nothing compared to what comes next. Shawn warns me that he is warming me up for the "good stuff". One house we visit is so popular we need to park a number of houses away as a large crowd has gathered. Every spare inch of the house and garden is covered in lights. There is no coherency, just splashes of colour, lights and blow-up figures everywhere. I'm pretty sure it is visible from the moon. This house is so over the top that their neighbours didn't even bother trying; they couldn't compete with this. Shawn and I snap a selfie and marvel at the creation.

"This is my favourite one," Shawn says, taking it all in as we watch the parents of young kids take their pictures next to some of the blow-up animals and light displays.

"It's chaotic but it kinda works," I agree.

"You can just tell they really love Christmas. It doesn't matter to them about creating something that matches or tells a story, it's just all there. You can just feel the joy coming from the place."

"Do you visit here every year?"

Shawn nods. "It's the same each time," he chuckles, "and you know what, if you go to the letterbox you'll find something else that's really cool."

I give him a confused smile, but he refuses to tell me anything more. Instead, he points to where a number of people are gathered around a brick letterbox at the end of the driveway. Shawn walks a step behind me and waits until I see what has him so excited. The owners of the home have a collection box set up outside their house with a note attached to a child-size, standing chalkboard.

"Thank you for visiting our Christmas lights. Many of the decorations you see have been collected over time, through our travels, bargained for by our children, or kindly donated by members of the community. We love Christmas, and we love sharing our display with you each year. To us, Christmas is a time to spend with those we love, share memories of those we've lost, and to look upon our

blessings both great and small. Every year our family donates funds to different charities. This year we have chosen to support the Indigenous Literacy Foundation. We ask that if you've enjoyed our display and would like to donate, please drop your contribution in the bucket below.
Merry Christmas, the Reid Family xo"

"The Reid family?" I say, looking over my shoulder at Shawn.

"This is my parent's house."

My mouth hangs open in delighted surprise. This is his *parent's house?* I thought Shawn took Christmas light hunting seriously – now I know why.

"How...?" I shake my head not knowing which question to ask first. "This is amazing. Oh my God, lucky I said I liked the display!"

We share a laugh, and I swear I see something more sparkle in his eyes.

"My parents have been doing this ever since I was a kid. We take turns picking a charity. It was my choice this year."

The choice of charity makes perfect sense for a primary school teacher. I'm speechless.

"Wait! You haven't even seen the best part yet." Shawn looks at the watch on his wrist and begins a countdown, to what I'm not entirely sure but as he says one, the lights all shut off for a moment. The large crowd murmurs before the sound of "Rockin' Around The Christmas Tree" blares through the night, and the lights flash in sync with the music. There are small cheers and gasps from the crowd, kids laugh and squeal with delight as they point at the lights.

"This is incredible!" I gasp, falling into Shawn's shoulder and instinctively wrapping my arm around his.

He doesn't move. He doesn't shift awkwardly. Instead he

looks down at me and smiles. There's something there behind those eyes, a look I haven't seen before. My lips tingle with anticipation, encouraging me to make a move, but I don't. Neither of us do. The memory of the almost-drunken kiss is still too fresh in my mind. Instead, I look at him, knowing my eyes are sparkling brightly right back at him.

Chapter Ten

Friday, 24th December – Birthday (and Christmas Eve, obviously)

Every Australian needs to have a pool or be friends with someone who does. After our Christmas lights tour last night, Shawn insists I join his family today by their pool and in their refrigerated, air-conditioned house. Since the temperature is already over thirty degrees by ten am, I don't need to be asked twice. I do, however, need a moment to gather myself before heading in. I try to convince myself that this is nothing more than a friend meeting another friend's family, but my heart betrays my mind and begins to race. I take five deep breathes to slow everything inside me down. This is just a swim, nothing more than an offer to keep cool on a ridiculously hot day. My phone rings, making me jump and my heart pick up pace again.

Dad. I smile and answer.

"Hello sweetheart, happy birthday!"

"Thanks, Dad."

"I just wanted to check in on you. It's going to be a hot one."

"I know. I'm actually at a friend's place today, hanging out by the pool."

"Oh good, good. Well, don't forget dinner is at six thirty tonight."

"I know Da–"

"Delilah, Holly's on the phone," he calls out. I can tell he's pulled the phone away slightly, but his voice is still loud, "come and say happy birthday."

"Why do I need to do that? I'll see her tonight. I'm so busy trying to get everything ready," Mum snaps in the background.

I roll my eyes, expecting nothing less. They continue to argue whilst I wait on the other end.

"You can spare a minute to say happy birthday. The caterers are fine..."

"Caterers?" I ask but Dad isn't listening.

"Just come...no, come on...Delilah!"

"Fine." I imagine Mum snatching the phone from Dad as her voice booms down the line, "Happy birthday, Holly. Don't forget dinner is at six thirty."

"I know. Dad said. Did I hear you hired caterers?"

"Oh yeah, it's just something for my blog. They want to work with me *blah blah blah*. Anyway, I have to go, I have a lot to organise. Don't forget to bring your special friend. Love you. Bye."

Before I could get another word in, she's gone and Dad is back on the line. "You there, Holly?"

"Yep, I'm here, Dad. Caterers?"

"Don't ask," he says, his voice dripping with annoyance. "So, who is this special friend?"

I slam my head back against the headrest of the driver's seat. "No one. There is no special friend, Dad."

"So, you're not bringing anyone tonight?"

"Nope."

"Huh."

I can hear Dad scratching at his chin through the line, his tell sign that he doesn't know what to say next. I save him from himself. "Well, anyway, I have to go."

"Yeah, yeah, of course. Happy birthday again, sweetheart."

"Thanks, Dad. I'll see you tonight."

"See you then."

He then says goodbye an obscene number of times before hanging up. At least my frustrating family had helped move my emotions around enough to feel settled and ready to walk into Shawn's family home. Only a small longing lingers in my stomach as I replay the words "special friend" over and over in my head. If only that could be true.

The door to the modern two-story house opens before I even get there, and I am greeted by a shirtless Shawn. Forget anything I said about feeling settled because fireworks are going off in every part of my body, and I swear I forget how to walk. I have never seen Shirtless Shawn before, Shirtless Shawn is buff. But not buff in the way that every muscle is painfully defined and on display; he just looks good. I can't stop my eyes from wandering as they take him all in.

"Happy birthday," he says, and I catch him smiling as my gaze finally finds his. *Happy birthday indeed.*

Words escape me so we work together in some form of pantomime. He swings the door further out and opens his arms, gesturing for me to enter. For reasons unbeknown to me, I curtsey as I pass him, and ever the good sport, Shawn replies with a bow. I wait for him as he closes the door, then lead the way into the house. He's moving funny. His back muscles seem tense, and I promise I'm only looking at them because I am a good friend concerned about his mental health...or something like that.

"Everyone's already out the back. Don't worry if you forget anyone's name," He says over his shoulder and gives me a smile I've never seen before but that I very much like.

I shrug my shoulders indifferently because I am incapable of speaking. We exit the open plan kitchen and living area into a well-manicured garden surrounding a crystal-clear pool dazzling in the sunlight. Music comes from a mysterious speaker and kids splash about. More shirtless men appear and women in bathing suits. No one here is self-conscious. No one is trying to take the perfect photo for a curated social media page. They're just a family enjoying each other's company. A twang of sadness pings in my chest.

"Everyone," Shawn puts on his yard duty voice and everyone looks his way. Heat suddenly rises to my cheeks. "This is Holly. Holly, everyone."

A wall of warm greetings and friendly smiles fly my way, and I can immediately pick out which two are his brothers. The three Reid boys all look the same, just varying by age. Shawn, despite being the youngest, actually looks bigger than his brothers in height and brawn. A woman in a stripped bikini and oversized glasses with her hair tied back in a messy bun approaches and wraps me in a familiar hug. "Nice to meet you. I'm Cait."

"Cait is a hugger," Shawn teases, and she playfully hits him on the arm as she loosens her embrace.

The two of them playfully bicker as I learn that Cait is married to Dane, the eldest Reid brother. They're high school sweethearts which Shawn mocks, but I can tell there is real affection underneath his comments. Cait drags me over to the sun lounge and introduces me to Jacinta and Terry – Shawn's parents. It's clear the boys get their looks from their mother with her beautiful jet-black hair and almond shaped eyes. My heart rate increases significantly as they warmly welcome me to their home. This is exactly the family I wish I had, and the welcome is doing very little to quieten any feelings I'm trying to squish down, deep inside, for Shawn. Okay, they're barely below surface level and it wouldn't be difficult to let them burst free. Still, I silently curse the whole family for being so unlike mine.

"We came past your light display last night. It was incredible," I say, taking a seat on a spare lounge.

"Why didn't you come in and say hi?" Jacinta asks.

I shrug and look at Shawn.

"We had other places to see."

Lies. We didn't go anywhere else after his parent's house. He took me home afterwards where we shared an awkward goodbye; one of those ones where it felt like there might be a kiss but we both leaned in for an awkward hug instead. Or maybe I made it awkward? I raise my eyebrows at him to let him know that I know he just lied to his mother and he lets a small smirk escape.

I fall into easy conversation with Shawn's parents and sister-in-law, so much so I don't even notice Shawn walk away. The Reid family laugh, poke fun at each other and seem genuinely interested in what I have to say. I'm left wondering if I ever have to leave to see my own family again.

The day flies by, and I find myself surrounded by Shawn's family in the pool, but he is nowhere in sight. I excuse myself to go and look for him. I grab my towel and quickly dry myself. Although Jacinta tells me not to worry about it, twenty-five – make that *twenty-six* – years of watching my every move under *Delilah-ful's* strict rules has me dry before entering the house. I immediately spot Shawn at the counter, lighting candles on what looks like an ice cream cake. "What are you doing?"

"Shoo! You're not supposed to see." He tries to cover the cake like a kid trying to cover their answers on a quiz. "I was going to bring it out to you by the pool."

My heart swells. "That thing will melt the second you step foot outside."

"Yeah, it's pretty hot."

"I feel like the surface of the sun would be a cooler place." We share a laugh, and he pushes the cake in front of me.

It's the Freddo frog ice cream cake, the one with hidden miniature chocolate frog heads inside. He's placed a pack of ten candles on top, and I want to jump in his arms and thank him.

"I can't tell you the last time I had ice cream cake."

"Reid family tradition. It's not a birthday without an ice cream cake."

"Shall we get everyone in?"

Shawn shakes his head. "It'll probably melt before they make it inside. I really didn't think this through."

I gently place my hand on his shoulder. "It's very thoughtful. Thank you."

"Happy birthday, Holly." He leans in, his lips lightly brushing my cheek, lingering there for a moment too long as if wondering if they should touch again.

"Cake!!" screams a voice from the door. It's Shawn's nephew Henry, and before I can blink, the whole family is inside singing Happy Birthday. Shawn gives me a small apologetic look that I can't help but smile at.

"Make a wish!" Henry demands.

I oblige Henry by closing my eyes, pretending to make a wish before blowing out the candles. In this moment, I can't think of anything I want more than what is right in front of me. Maybe that's the wish, to make all of this actually mine. The Reid family have been so welcoming that it's hard to remember that I don't really have a place here. At least, not in the way I'd like.

"What was the wish?"

Cait, holding up her nephew at the bench, gasps. "She can't tell us, Henry."

"Then it won't come true?" he asks, eyes wide as if he's just discovered the meaning of life.

"Exactly." Cait bops him on the nose.

"You have to cut it," Henry shouts.

"And if it comes out dirty, you have to kiss the nearest boy!" Shawn's niece Molly squeals with delight.

"Uncle Shawn is the closest!" Henry matches her enthusiasm.

I take the knife and try my best to make it look like I'm cutting it carefully to avoid kissing their uncle, but really, I'm moving it from side to side in order to make it come out messy. When I pull the knife out, a clump of ice cream sticks to it. The children squeal wildly, and I play up to them.

"You have to kiss Uncle Shawn!" Molly shouts, pointing her finger at us.

I sheepishly look at Shawn.

"It's okay, you don't have to," he mumbles discreetly.

"But it's the rules!" Molly shouts even louder.

"Okay, okay." I put the knife down and stand on my tippy toes to kiss Shawn on the cheek. Quick. Casual. And deeply unsatisfying. What I want to do to him right now is certainly not fit for young innocent eyes.

"On the lips!" Molly exclaims as Cait lifts her up and away.

"Alright," she says, "that's about enough out of you." She gives us both a sympathetic look and hurries to change the subject, whilst Shawn's brothers and brother-in-law chuckle to themselves. I can feel the heat radiating off my face. "If you want ice cream you have to sit at the table."

Shawn takes over cutting duties as the four kids race to get their seats.

"They'll do anything for ice cream." Cait waggles her eyebrows at me.

I look over at Shawn who managed to tie his hair back when I wasn't looking, and I'll be damned if I've ever seen him look more handsome than right now, laser-focused on cutting up an ice cream cake – my ice cream cake – and making sure everyone gets an even amount. It is in this moment I realise I'm a goner. I've completely fallen head over heels for my best friend, and it's going to cause me a world of pain.

Chapter Eleven

Friday, 24ᵗʰ December – Birthday, and Christmas Eve

I easily lose track of time. After eating the ice cream cake, we settle on the couch to watch *The Grinch*, and Shawn and I continually quote the movie. The kids think we're movie buff superheroes for knowing all the words while the adults think we're just plain annoying. It's not until after the film that I realise the time. Six o'clock. I inwardly curse. I won't have time to go home to shower and change before I need to be at Mum and Dad's house for dinner. It shouldn't matter. It is just the family, but I know my just-come-from-the-pool look will not please *Delilah-ful*. I thank Jacinta and Terry for having me, and Shawn agrees to walk me out.

"Why do you have to go?" Henry pouts.

"Can't she just stay forever?" Molly crosses her arms and joins her cousin pouting from the couch.

Cait's husband Dane scoops them up. "You lot better have a bath and get ready for bed if you want Santa to come in the morning."

I have completely forgotten it's Christmas Eve. The Reid

family have not mentioned Christmas once today, instead, focusing their attention on me and my birthday. Suddenly, I feel bad about taking up their day. I say my goodbyes while Cait reminds me about tonight. "You are coming to see Dane play tonight, aren't you?"

"Yep, I'll be there. I might pop home to shower and change first though."

"I wouldn't worry about it. Most people will stumble in from the beach anyway on a night like this," Dane bellows as he juggles two wriggling kids.

Shawn stops himself from saying something. Instead, he covers his thoughts with a tight smile and ushers me to the front door. Before opening it, he reaches into a woven basket sitting under a hall table and pulls out a neatly wrapped gift with a bow on it.

"What's this?" I ask as he sheepishly hands it to me.

"I believe it's this new thing called a gift," he smirks.

I shake my head at him and unwrap the present. Underneath the bright, happy birthday paper is a small brown leather back-pack with tassels hanging off it. I let out an involuntary gasp. The leather is the softest thing I have ever laid my hands on.

"This is beautiful. You really didn't have too." But I'm so glad he did.

"I wanted to. I remember you saying you wanted one from that market we took the kids to for their inquiry project."

That was five months ago! We had taken our grades to the local Main Street markets for their maths inquiry project. Had he really remembered all this time?

"Thank you." I want to tell him that I'm surprised he remembered. I want to tell him that he's one of the very few people to buy me a real birthday present in all my twenty-six years. I want to tell him I'm falling in love with him; but I don't say any of it. Instead, he reaches down and wraps me in his arms, kissing the top of my head.

"Happy birthday, Hol."

Chapter Twelve

Friday, 24ᵗʰ December – Christmas Eve

I don't really remember getting to Mum and Dad's. I know I drove there. I'm pretty sure I followed the road rules, but my mind was elsewhere, namely back at the Reid family home snuggled up next to Shawn. In the short twenty-minute drive (although it was really thirty -five minutes thanks to holiday traffic and one-way roads) I lived the most delicious life with Shawn in my imagination, and it left me feeling hollow. The man I want yet can't have.

I think about what he is doing now, counting down the minutes until I see him again tonight at his brother's show. My heart aches more now that I have met his family and seen how seamlessly I could fit into his world. But I am here, in my world, with my family and...a hell of a lot of cars. I have to park five houses down from my parent's because the street parking is taken up. I'd like to think their neighbours are hosting large family get togethers but as I approach Mum and Dad's house, the sound of festive music and jolly voices travels through the front gate, and I just know that these cars are here for *Delilah-ful*. It instantly puts me in a bad mood. I stalk through the front door. As expected, people buzz about my parent's home, and I barely recognise any of them. I see Jesse and his very pregnant wife, Bridie, sitting on the couch watching the scene unfold around them. I greet them both with a quick kiss on the cheek.

"What's going on?" I wave my hands around the room.

"*Delilah-ful* is what's going on," Jesse says with distain.

"Happy birthday, Holly," Bridie smiles. I thank her before pressing my brother for more information.

"She wanted to thank everyone for their hard work during the year."

I roll my eyes. That's not how Dad had made it seem. "So, this is an end-of-year-Christmas-party, not a birthday dinner?" I clarify.

Bridie's apologetic smile tells me everything I need to know, and all I can do is wish myself elsewhere. Of course, she couldn't let me have this one day. She couldn't just let me have my day. She had to make it about her and her stupid blog.

"She's gonna be pissed when she sees you dressed like that," Jesse points over his whiskey glass at my poolside ensemble.

I shrug my shoulders indifferently. The string from my black bikini top is visible underneath the stripy maxi dress I've thrown on. My hair, which is screaming out for a brush, is thrown into a bird's nest of a bun on top of my head, and I smell like chlorine. The complete opposite of the designer clothes and layers of make-up swanning around me.

"We gotcha something but I left it at home, so I'll give it to you tomorrow," he follows up.

Of course he has. "Did you know all these people were coming?"

Jesse and Bridie shake their heads. "Nah. If I had of known I wouldn't have dragged Bridie here. She's uncomfortable enough as it is."

"Honestly, it's fine." She rests her hand on his arm, but I can see the tiredness in her eyes.

The doctors have already told her that the baby is measuring big, and on Bridie's tiny little frame, I can only imagine what that must feel like. Jesse's eyes flame with anger, and I wonder how many whiskeys he's had.

"Where's Layla?" I ask, trying to change the topic. Jesse shrugs. "Is she coming?"

Another shrug. My brother isn't big on words at the best of times, let alone when he's really angry. He'd rather sit in the corner and shoot daggers at you with his eyes all evening. He's a giant sook but at least he's not making a scene.

"We're giving it thirty more minutes."

"What? And then you're leaving? What about the food?"

"Mum's already said it's running late. It's too hot to deal with this crap. Plus, she wants everyone to sit outside so she's holding out for the cool change."

"What cool change? The forecast is hot forever," I complain.

The last thing I want to do is leave the cool indoors for the hot, sticky, fly-ridden outdoors, crammed next to strangers while I pretend to enjoy their end-of-year work party. I excuse myself to get a drink and find my parents. I find Dad first who gives me a kiss and wishes me a happy birthday again. He can't stay and chat because he has Things To Do. I find Mum, the centre of attention, surrounded by people who look at her like she's some sort of domestic goddess when in actual fact, she hasn't lifted a finger; not with the decorations, not with the food and not with her own children. But she throws her arms around me and makes a big motherly display about how excited she is that I have finally arrived.

"What are you wearing?" she whispers in my ear as she pulls me in for a hug and then plasters on a fake smile again as we pull apart.

"I've been by the pool." I resist the automatic urge to apologise to her.

She and her followers let out a laugh that says *kids, am I right?* Like I'm some small child who can't be taken seriously.

"Can I speak to you for a moment?"

She excuses herself and we find the study vacant. As soon as she shuts the door, her expression changes to annoyance.

"What is it? I have guests. I need to mingle."

"I thought this was supposed to be a family dinner for my birthday?"

"Oh, Holly, come on. Is this what *this* is about?" She waves her hands over me as if my wardrobe is a declaration of war against her.

"I–"

"Holly, you are twenty-seven years old. You are not a child any more. I don't need to throw you any birthday parties."

"I'm twenty-six," I grumble.

"Oh, well, good for you. A year younger. Look, it's very important that I show these people how hospitable we can be, so they continue to work with me and promote my work. This is how the whole thing works, Holly. Surely you can understand that."

"What about me? It's my birthday, the one–"

"Holly, love, the world doesn't revolve around you. It's Christmas tomorrow, and we can celebrate then. A huge family celebration at your brand-new home."

The fact that she chooses now to call my place "home" is not lost on me.

"I have a cake for tonight, and we can sing you happy birthday but please be reasonable. It's a little bit embarrassing that a woman in her late twenties is throwing a tantrum about not getting a birthday party." She pats my shoulder. "Are we done? I have people I need to speak to."

I nod. There's so much more I want to say, but I know it will just fall upon deaf ears. Maybe she's right. Maybe I am too old to care so much about celebrating my birthday. But then I think back to how everything was this afternoon with Shawn and his family, and they had no problems in celebrating my day. Did they think I was being a big baby about it? Were they only celebrating it because Shawn told them to appease me? No, the Reid family aren't like that. I wish I was with them right now.

Needing some air, I go outside to the street and see a number of families outside waving as the local fire brigade drive one of their fire trucks down the street, throwing out lollies to the kids, and spraying water on them. I take a picture of it and send it to Shawn.

H: Your nieces and nephews would have loved this.

He sends back a picture of pretty much the same thing.

S: They came here too. Tradition.
　　H: How many lollies did you score?
　　S: All of them. They're the hard ones so the kids aren't interested. Lol! How's your bday dinner?
　　H: Going swell. Just us and about 35 of Delilah-fuls nearest and dearest staff. *eye roll emoji*
　　S: That sucks! Bail. Come back here.
　　H: I should. I'll just catch you later at the bar.
　　S: Was just about to message you about that. CANCELLED. Blackout at the venue.

I wanted to cry but I didn't let Shawn know that.

H: What? Oh no! That sucks!
　　S: I'm kinda glad though, too hot to move.

I try not to let the disappointment settle in my chest.

Breathe in, breathe out.

Thunder breaks out in the distance, and I look up to see a storm sweeping along the horizon of the ocean. I guess *Delilah-ful* will get her wish, the cool change with a storm that looks like it will pass right by. She can have her Insta-worthy, picture-perfect Christmas break-up party after all. As I look around at the families mingling in the street and watching the fire truck slowly make its way around the corner, I realise that I don't want to be here. I flip back through Shawn's messages, and it suddenly hits me like a freight train – I don't have to be here. If Jesse and Bridie get to bail, and Layla doesn't even have to show up, why should I stick around? It's my birthday and I should be doing whatever I want.

Chapter Thirteen

Friday, 24ᵗʰ December – Christmas Eve

Turns out, sitting in front of my fans and eating ice-cream straight from the tub is what I want to be doing on my birthday. Flicking through the channels, I by-pass the holiday movies, all of which are set in the American winter which makes me especially angry this year. I can't help but smile as I turn to look at my very Australian Christmas tree, decorated in troves of colour and hideous Australiana ornaments. This very moment – the ice cream, the tree, the quiet – is all a reminder that I don't have to do what is expected of me. In celebration of my newly acquired sense of freedom, I finish the tub of ice cream and stream *10 Things I Hate About You*.

Just as I reach the paintball scene, there is a knock at my door. To my surprise, Shawn stands on the other side of it.

"What are you doing here?" I say, moving to the side to allow him to come in.

He does but we don't move from the doorway. "When you said you were just coming back home to have a quiet evening, I felt bad. It's your birthday! And Christmas Eve. No one should be alone on either of those days."

"But you live alone." I point out to him.

"Yes, but I always spend Christmas Eve at my parents' house."

An image of the whole Reid family in matching pyjamas flashes through my mind, and it's almost too much.

"No," he says, his lips twitching.

"No, what?"

"I can hear you wondering if we wear matching pyjamas. No, we don't."

"How did you–"

"One, because I know you, and, two, I just feel like it would be something you were made to do as a child."

I grin. "Have you been checking out *Delilah-ful's* page? She posted a flashback last week. Matching pjs and all."

"I haven't but I will now." He pulls out his phone and immediately scrolls onto her page, pulling up said photo. "That is hideous."

He doubles taps the image, and then shows it to me. I know it frighteningly well. Not only are we in matching blue and white Christmas onesies, but my sister and I have matching braids. She is holding a Minnie Mouse Christmas teddy while I hold Mickey. I remember it vividly because it was the beginning of my Minnie Mouse obsession which lasted until I was twelve, and Layla, who never really liked stuffed teddies, threw such a tantrum because she wanted to hold "the girl one". I was left holding Mickey after being told off for deliberately being difficult and making my sister cry. Funny how she immediately stopped crying once she had the damn mouse in a dress.

"You should try and re-create this Christmas photo next year." Shawn jokes.

"I'm permanently scarred. Do you want to come in, or are you attached to my front door for some reason?"

Shawn shifts on the spot. "Ah, yeah, sure."

We flop down onto the couch and I press play on the remote.

We fall easily into random small talk, and I forget to pay attention to the rest of the movie.

The movie isn't the only thing we aren't paying attention too. Time also appears to flash by.

"Oh wow! It's after midnight," I say as my smart watch buzzes to remind me to move.

"Well then...Merry Christmas," Shawn smiles.

"Merry Christmas." I smile back, and we do this weird lean in wondering if the other person wants to hug or not.

Our arms clamp around each other, and I feel my shoulders relax. Balancing on my knees, I'm concerned about falling into his lap until his stubble rubs against that sweet spot just below my ear. His breath is warm, and we stay like this for what seems like forever. I'm waiting for him to make the move he is so desperately teasing he will make. But he doesn't. We pull apart, and I can't help but be disappointed. Shawn gets up from the couch and goes to my Christmas tree, moving aside presents as if looking for something.

"Um, I didn't get you anything if that's what you're looking for." Lies. I have, and it's on my phone. He'll positively nerd out when I send it to him. I can't wait!

He doesn't respond. Instead, he pulls a small present wrapped in white and red paper from under the tree. I don't recognise the paper or the size of the present. I think back to what I bought for my family, and nothing this small comes to mind.

"Here," he holds the gift out in front of me, "I stashed it here the other day. Merry Christmas, Holly."

I look at him, at that warm, heart-melting smile, and it takes all of my strength to just sit here and not jump up and wrap my whole body around his.

"Two in less than twelve hours," I mock. "You didn't have to," I say taking the gift and carefully peeling back the sticky tape so as not to rip the wrapping. "Did you wrap this yourself?"

He nods. Of course he did. It's perfectly wrapped. It has his name all over it. My heart thunders in my chest as I see the familiar teal box of a very expensive jewellery chain. I gasp. I look to Shawn and see that his whole body has tensed, and he looks like he's holding his breath, waiting for my approval.

"Shawn...," I whisper, and he crouches down in front of me.

I pull out a necklace from inside the box. It's a signature Tiffany heart and key pendant on a chain, and I turn it over in my hands. I've never owned anything this beautiful before.

"Is it okay? I wasn't sure if..." he leaves his words hanging in the air between us.

"It's perfect. I'm speechless. But...I...I thought you only bought presents for family at Christmas time?"

His cheeks flush and his lips curl into a lopsided grin, one I've never seen on him before but one I like very much. "Holly, you are my family. My chosen family." He reaches for my hands to take the necklace from them and carefully places it around my neck. "Maybe one day...my real family."

Tears well in my eyes unexpectedly. "So which brother do I have to marry then?"

We share a laugh. He finally looks up at me through his lashes, and I fall into his big brown eyes. "I had no idea." My words come out as barely a whisper. I'm still unsure if I am somehow misreading the whole situation.

"Yeah, well, I can be pretty secretive when I want to be. I call it self-preservation."

"You never need to do that with me."

He nods. "I know. I had this whole big speech that I was going to give, cliché and all, about you having the key to my heart," he fingers the necklace, "and you were supposed to find the present on Christmas Day, and then call me. That way if you hated it, I didn't have to be witness to it and—"

"I don't hate it," I interject as I suddenly realise I haven't said much at all about the necklace. "I love it. Thank you."

He gives a curt nod, satisfied that he did something right. He rubs the palms of his hands along his shorts.

"So...about this big speech and key to your heart part..."

"You're really gonna make me do it?" The red in his cheeks deepens as he takes a deep breath, already knowing the answer to his own questions. He clears his throat, "Holly."

"Good start."

"Thank you," he winks. "Holly, I, um, okay. Wow, this is harder than I thought it would be."

"Just breathe." I mimic breathing in and out, and his mischievous grin returns. "It's just me you're talking to."

"That's the hard part," he lets out a short breathy laugh, "I just wanted this to be perfect, and now I'm forgetting everything I wanted to say."

"Then just say whatever." I try to remain calm and refrain from declaring my undying love for him, knowing that this is the most romantic moment of my life – ever!

"I like you." He points to me and I giggle. "I like you, and I was too scared to say anything because I didn't want to ruin our friendship. And then spending all this time together doing Christmas things...I just missed you when I wasn't with you. I kinda wanted everything to keep going wrong, so you'd keep asking me for help," He chuckles, and I playfully knock him in the shoulder as if I am offended by his comment. "I know! I know! I was going to tell you the other night when we went to see the lights, but then I chickened out, so I planned on telling you tonight at the pub, but then that was cancelled, and I thought it was the universe's way of telling me not to saying anything until Cait essentially told me to stop being a big scaredy cat and do it."

"Scaredy cat?"

"The kids were still awake."

We smile at each other, and he takes my hands in his. "If this is all too much or, or you don't feel the same–"

"No, no! Not at all. I mean, not *not* at all. I mean, yes, I do. I'm just...confused," I say hurriedly, "I thought you didn't like me because of that night at Gregor's party." I don't want to say it out loud but from the blank look on his face, I'm going to have to relive the horror. "The kiss? Well, the almost kiss. I tried to kiss you, and you rejected me."

He rolls his head. "Oh that! You were drunk, and I didn't want to take advantage of you. Trust me, I wanted too, but up until that point, I had no idea that you were vaguely interested in me. I didn't want you regretting it the next day!"

"Vaguely interested? Oh my God, Shawn, I couldn't have been any more obvious! Even the kids at school were teasing me." I laugh.

"I honestly had no idea. I mean, I hoped, but I just thought you were being nice to me because I was the experienced teacher next door." He shakes his head.

"You make me sound like some teaching minx."

"Think of all this time we've wasted."

I shuffle closer towards him and lean forward. This time, he completely understands and closes the gap between us. He cups my face as his lips softly meet mine, tenderly moving them apart and kissing me deeply. Fireworks explode in every part of my body, making me feel alive. I can't believe we let this whole year go by without kissing like this for every single one of those days.

"What now?" I whisper.

"Whatever we want."

Chapter Fourteen

Christmas Day

The cool change doesn't last long. In fact, it's boiling by the time I say goodbye to Shawn and jump in the shower, readying myself for a day of festivities. I've seen a lot of today already, and it has barely begun. My birthday, which started out great, went bad and ended wonderfully, is but a long distant memory as I try to pull off the best Christmas lunch ever on very little sleep. Although I know he'll be back tonight, I'm already missing Shawn. Urgh, are we going to be *that* couple? Gross. My fingers find the pendant hanging around my neck and I absent-mindedly twirl it between them, as my cheeks flush thinking about last night.

Walking to the kitchen, I gasp, standing in front of the fridge. The absence of a turkey in there shakes me out of my Shawn daydream. But not enough to stops me from texting him.

H: MAYDAY! MAYDAY! I forgot to take the turkey out of the freezer!

S: It needs at least a day to defrost!

H: Where was this advice a day ago?! I'm so screwed.

S: I realise this isn't the time for crude jokes so I'll let this PERFECT opportunity pass...

H: How very gentlemanly of you. WHAT AM I GOING TO DO?!

S: What else do you have?

H: Vegetables to roast and chocolate Bavarian in the freezer.

S: Is that all?! I'm concerned.

H: I only bought the essentials for Christmas. My tiny fridge can't hold much!

S: OK, we're going fridge hunting in the Boxing Day sales.

H: Sweet, but doesn't help me now! Crisis mode.

S: The shops aren't open...

H: Neither is the fish market because EVERYONE is smarter than me and is prepared. I am a monumental stuff up. And this will be just the thing Delilah-ful will secretly love because it will show her that I. Cannot. Adult!!

S: Deep breath. Look, we always have more than enough here. What if I just drop some extras off?

H: I can't ask you to do that.

S: You didn't.

H: Shawn...I can't take food from your family. It will be fine. It's like, hotter than the sun in here. Maybe the turkey will thaw in time.

S: Sorry, can't hear you. Collecting supplies.

H: That's not how text messages work.

S: I'll be at yours in twenty. Pre heat the oven.

H: You CANNOT take food from your family!!

S: OVEN. PRE HEAT.180.

H: Shawn, don't bother... My power just went out.

My phone screams to life, and I know it's him without even looking. I slide my thumb across the bottom of the screen and lift the phone to my ear as I stare into the fridge whose light has gone. *Same fridge, same.*

"Are you joking? It's really hard to tell in a text."

"I wish," I sigh. "Everything has just suddenly stopped."

"Did you check the fuse?"

"I don't even know what that is!"

"Okay, don't panic," Shawn's deep voice is hypnotic as I watch my perfect Christmas go up in smoke before my eyes. Not literal smoke of course, although at this stage nothing would surprise me.

His voice guides me outside to the power box where I see a row of switches. All of them are facing up. Shawn confirms my suspicions; it's a blackout. I look around and see the other residents of the unit block, all checking their fuse boxes too.

"Merry bloody Christmas!" Mr Jones at number four waves to me.

"I hope it won't take long to fix," I say back to him.

Mr Jones says, "Don't hold your breath love" just as Shawn says, "It's unlikely to be fixed soon" down the line.

"I'm off to my daughter's place anyway. Have a good one." He nods and retreats back inside.

"What am I going to do?" I say down the phone to Shawn. "This is just so typical."

"It's not like it's your fault. Give the power company a call and see what can be done. The system is probably just overloaded with all these hot days."

"Do you have power?"

"I refuse to answer that question." He says it with a smile in his voice, but it still makes me let out a sound like a strangled cat. "Wait, I think I may have an idea. Give me twenty minutes."

I don't bother arguing. At this point, whatever he can come up with will be a huge improvement on offering my family raw vegetables and a melted Bavarian cake.

Chapter Fifteen

Christmas Day

Shawn arrives before the rest of my family. The pretty dress I bought especially for today is a distance thought as I throw on a pair of shorts and a loose tee, and bundle my hair into a messy bird's nest of a bun. It's becoming my signature look. It's at this time every year that I contemplate shaving my head, and as for make up? Forget it. It will melt off my face in five minutes flat. The only thing I bother to make sure I'm wearing is the necklace that Shawn gifted me; and to be honest, I haven't taken it off. I still can't believe last night even happened.

"What is that?" I hold the side gate open as Shawn carries through a black dome.

"A Weber."

"Shawn, I don't even know how to use a BBQ let alone a weber. Don't you need those black things?"

"Coals? No, this runs on a gas bottle."

While I stare down the small domed BBQ like the foreign object it is, Shawn makes a return trip to the car bringing in a small gas bottle and a cold bag. I open it to find an uncooked chicken inside.

"Before you say anything, this is a spare chook that we aren't using today."

"Who has a spare roast chicken lying around?" I know the answer as I ask the question.

Shawn, ever the gentleman, doesn't say what we're both thinking: *prepared adults, Holly, that's who!*

"Mum was going to cook it later in the week. I'll just pop down and grab one when the shops open again tomorrow." He shrugs like it's no big deal that he has just saved my entire Christmas.

"*I* will pop down and grab one. I'll grab two, to say thank you to your mum for saving the day."

"It's fine. It's not as if *she* lugged this big thing here all by herself...," he flashes a mischievous grin.

"Is this your way of asking me what *your* thank you is, Mr Reid?"

Sensing my playful tone, he stops assembling the gas to the weber and pulls me closer to him. "I mean, I did it out of the goodness of my own heart, but if you have something else in mind...."

We kiss and for a brief moment, I feel all my troubles melt away.

"Well actually, since you ask, I *do* have something for you." I pull out my phone and flick the confirmation email across to Shawn's phone.

"No way," he says excitedly as he opens the message, "two tickets to the Moonlight cinema *Star Wars* trilogy marathon!"

"A picnic dinner is included as well as two deck chairs and drinks."

"But it says two." He waggles his eyebrows at me. I know what's coming.

"You can choose to take whoever you want."

"What if I want to take you? A picnic kinda sounds romantic. Might be weird if I take Dane."

We share a laugh. "I know you don't really like *Star Wars*, but it would kinda be nice to take my *girlfriend*, with me."

He says the word with such hesitation, as if he's still unsure about how I might react to the word. Little does he know I'll do anything to keep him calling me that forever. Okay, forever might be too long, one day it should be wife. *Whoa! Slow down, Holly.*

"I'd like that," I say with a smile and kiss him again.

The kissing doesn't last nearly as long as I would like it to as Shawn very seriously walks me through how to use the Weber to roast the chicken and vegetables. I wish he could stay, but I couldn't put him through my family today, or any other day really. Is it at all possible to marry someone and create a life with them without them having to meet or interact with your family? Asking for a friend.

I also couldn't bear to take him away from his family for another second. He's already done so much for me.

"Still on for later?" I suggest in between goodbye kisses by the car.

"Already counting down."

We peel apart, and I watch him drive out of the shared driveway just as I see my father's car pull in. Of course they're the first to arrive – and early. I'm sure *Delilah-ful* is itching to give my disaster a once over before she demands we all go back to her house, where she will no doubt already have a turkey slow cooking in the oven. You know, just in case.

"Hello, sweetheart." She swans over to me dressed like she's just stepped out of her blog pages – think white linen everything, red lipstick, and her dark hair perfectly styled into a sleek pony tail.

After the driveway greetings, I take them inside where she looks around, assessing my decorating. I set the table last night with matching crockery and my finest cutlery – I'm kidding; I only have one type of cutlery, I just made sure it looked extra shiny. I even used the name cards Shawn made for me. I am pretty proud of my efforts and she must be too because she doesn't say much.

"You really stuck with the Australiana theme," she muses, picking up the place cards with watercolour drawings of Australian animals dressed in Christmas hats.

"A fair dinkum Aussie Christmas," Dad smiles, hands on hips. "I haven't had one of those since I was a little tacker."

Mum gives Dad The Look. She hates when he lets his Australian-ness slip out.

"Hell-oo," I hear Bridie as she makes her way in, followed by my brother carrying armfuls of presents.

Bridie greets my parents first as is custom in our house before wrapping her arms around me and whispering in my ear, "You did good, Hol."

"Geez, it's bloody hot in here, Hol. Reckon it's cooler outside. You gonna put the aircon on or what?" This is how Jesse greets me and it's time to break the news to them all.

"Funny you should mention that." I clasp my hands, rubbing them together. Are they sweaty? Or am I just sweaty? I don't know the difference anymore. "So, my aircon packed up the other day. I had some idiot out who said he couldn't fix it until the new year, and then this morning, this will really make you laugh, my power went out."

I wait for a chuckle or two, but all I get is an awkward laugh from dad.

"But don't worry," I rush to reassure the shocked looking relatives staring at me, "my...friend came to the rescue and I have a Weber going outside."

I decide not to disclose that Shawn and I are together. It's just one thing too much to handle today.

"Well, then, good thinking, Holly love. Can't say I've ever had a turkey in the Weber."

"Actually, Dad, it's a chook."

Another moment of silence passes before Dad awkwardly

breaks it, "Ah well, that will be alright. It doesn't really matter does it? As long as we're all together, that's the main thing."

Mum doesn't say anything, but Bridie backs up Dad and puts a positive spin on the day. "Way to save the day, Holly. Love the Australian theme you have going on." She flashes me a sincere smile and heads out the back.

"Way to ruin the day, Hol." Jesse clasps my shoulder as he walks past and follows his wife outside.

I notice Mum doesn't say anything. She merely smiles and follows the others outside.

"Have I ruined Christmas? It's not the big flashy day everyone is used to," I say to Dad.

He wraps his arms around me and plants a kiss on my fore-head. "I prefer this any day of the week, Hol."

"But Mum goes so overboard with everything."

"Don't worry about Mum. She'll have a great day, love. You did good, kid."

"Thanks, Dad. She hasn't even commented on my outfit yet." I say as we walk outside together just as Mum turns to me and says, "Are you getting changed Holly?"

Dad and I share a knowing look and before I can give my answer, Layla walks through to the back with – The Christmas Ruiner?

He doesn't look half as surprised as I am to see him in my house again. Does he have the part I am missing? Seems a little strange to deliver it on Christmas Day, not that there's much point with the power being out and all.

"Hi everyone," Layla sings.

I walk past her and straight to the Christmas Ruiner. "Did the part come in? I didn't think you'd deliver it on Christmas Day."

"Not exactly," he smiles smugly and shoves his hands in the pockets of his jeans. Jeans! On this day of fire.

"I don't understand,"

I hear Mum squeal and spin around to see her and Bridie bent over Layla's outstretched hand. Everything moves in slow motion as I take in the scene around me. "I don't understand." I repeat.

Layla glides over to me and shoves her hand in my face where a giant pear-shaped diamond sparkles back at me. "Connor and I are engaged!" she squeals excitedly.

"Where is Connor?" I ask, and everyone looks at me like they're just as confused as I feel.

"Um, hi." I spin around to see the Christmas Ruiner behind me waving.

"Sorry, yes, the air conditioner..."

"No, *I'm* Connor," he says and points to the ring as if to say that he's responsible for the thing on my sister's finger.

I look between my sister and the Christmas Ruin...Connor... and it takes a moment before my brain computes. It must be over-heating like the rest of the earth today. "What?"

"Oh, Holly, don't be so rude. You should congratulate your sister. We're all so happy for the two of you." Mum coos towards Layla and wraps her in another hug.

Suddenly, arms and back slaps are flying everywhere as "congratulations" rings through the air.

"This is why we didn't make it last night," Layla goes on to explain, "Connor had decorated his house so beautifully. Oh! You should have seen the tree!"

I give Connor my filthiest side eyes as my sister continues, "Anyway, it was so pretty and perfect. Connor got down on one knee, and I said yes, and then we wanted to celebrate just the two of us, and well, you know," she hints, and I don't think we need to hear any more.

"I don't understand. How did...when did...we're all okay with Layla getting engaged to a guy none of us have met before?"

"We've met him," Jesse returns.

"Yesterday morning," Bridie chips in apologetically.

"He's been to our house a number of times." Mum stands tall. "Honestly, Holly, what has gotten into you?"

"Probably mad little sis got the carat before she did," Jesse snorts, and Bridie slaps him on the arm for me.

I give her a look that says thank you. "Wait, am I the only one who hasn't met Connor?"

"Well, that's not technically true," Connor intervenes with what I imagine to be a charming smile as it appears to work on everyone but me.

"Yes," Layla giggles, "Connor told me when we rocked up that he was here trying to fix your aircon the other day. Small world."

"Did he also tell you he stole my Christmas tree and turkey?"

Dad looks at me confused. "I thought we were having chicken?"

"The heat must be getting to her," Bridie offers, "let's go in and get a cold drink, huh?" She practically pushes me through the door, and I do not envy her future child. She is no push over, despite her small frame.

"Here," she hands me a glass of tap water that is warm, but I gulp it down anyway. "You good?"

"It's been a long week," I muse and slump down on a leatherback stool at the island bench.

"Look, I know how difficult today has been for you. Trying to live up to Delilah's expectations is not easy on anyone. But you've done a good job. Despite everything going on with the power and all, you've done it!"

I look around at my small little unit, proud of what I have managed to throw together in a week. It may not feel like a *Delilah-ful* Christmas, but it does feel like a *Holly Jolly Christmas*, and that is more than enough.

"You're right."

"I know," she smiles at me playfully, "look, sit back, relax and enjoy the day. Next year we'll have a little one to run around after and I'm sure no one will be able to have anything nice out because he will destroy it all."

"He?" My ears prick up.

"Merry Christmas, Aunt Holly," Bridie smiles, and I immediately wrap her in my arms.

"Please tell me I'm not the last to know."

She shakes her head with a huge grin on her face. "You're the first to know. Jesse and I have made these little gender reveal things for everyone, so you have to act surprised when he gives it to you."

I run my fingers across my lips as if I am zipping them closed. "Promise."

I crouch down and run a hand over Bridie's belly with her permission. "I already love you so much, little man."

"He loves you too. He kicks a lot when he hears your voice."

"That's because he knows I'm the fun aunty."

Bridie doesn't correct me because she knows it's true, and we go back outside to be with the others.

Chapter Sixteen

Christmas Day

I almost die of shock when *Delilah-ful* offers me a compliment after lunch and everyone raises their glasses to toast the host. *Me.*

"Holly, congratulations on a delightful Christmas in your new home," Mum says, and I stare at her for a moment, waiting for the follow up insult that never comes. Strange.

"Thank you?" I say carefully.

"I'm surprised you know how to cook on a Weber."

I smile into my glass and mumble, "I'm surprised you know what one is," before turning to Connor and adding, "you can't steal that."

My family look at me like I'm mad, but Connor just shrugs it off. I'm not entirely sure how I feel about him yet. He hasn't said much throughout the day although he does look at my sister like she has rainbows shooting out of her, which is both gross and endearing.

We bring the gifts outside as Jesse is right, it is cooler outside than in, and that's saying something because it still feels like we haven't left the surface of the sun for days. We're protected by a large tree in the backyard that gives off shade and is the most pleasant spot on the whole property. As I sit there watching even the hardest of hearts unwrap and appreciate gifting, I wonder if I could throw some fairy lights in the tree and sit out here of an evening enjoying a wine and a book.

Layla gives Mum and Dad the Santa photo which prompts laughter all around. I swear I even see Mum's eyes sparkle a bit like there are actual tears in them. She doesn't let one drop, but I can see she loves the photo. Of course, she gives Layla the credit and like any younger sibling, she takes it all for herself, but I don't correct her. Just knowing they love it is enough for me.

Jesse is next to hand out gifts, and each one of us receive the same sized white box with red and green ribbon. I join the others in looking around like I'm trying to figure out what this gift could possibly be when I catch Bridie's eye, and she gives me a little wink.

Layla must sense something because like me, she's slowed down the unwrapping to let Mum and Dad be the first to discover the present. They gasp as they hold up a black and white sonogram with a pair of blue booties. Mum definitely has tears in her eyes now. Layla and I unwrap our boxes. Ours comes with a sonogram picture too, along with a onesie that says 'I'm my auntie's favourite" in blue writing.

"A boy? You're having a boy?" Mum manages to get out before the first tear falls.

"We're having a boy!" Bridie shouts, and we have another round of hugs, back slaps and congratulations.

"Have you thought about a name? I've always liked–"

"Mum," Jesse warns.

"What? I was just trying to–"

"We know. We know. We have a name already picked out."

Layla and I share a quick glance. *Wrong answer, Jesse.* Mum's eyes grow wider in anticipation.

"Nope," Jesse shakes his head. "That is all you get. You'll know his name when he's born and not a moment before."

"Oh come on, Jesse, that's cruel. Just give me a letter so I can have some special blankets made up. Oh and I could get–"

"No!" we all say in unison, except for Connor, who's rightfully chosen not to get involved.

"Why don't you bother Layla? I'm sure she could use your help in planning the wedding." Jesse smirks knowing he has just thrown Layla under a metaphorical bus.

She narrows her eyes at him. "Thank you, *brother*."

"Actually, you've done such a smashing job with Christmas, Holly, maybe you'd like to take over planning duties," Connor says to me as the others fight over who's getting involved in whose business.

"At least this time I won't have someone stealing my things at every turn."

"I don't know what you're referring to."

"It makes sense though. You stole my Christmas, and now you've stolen my sister and my family."

Connor chuckles. "And she's about to steal my last name. I call it even. Look, I'm sorry about the way I acted this last week. I know how much Christmas means to Layla, and I just wanted everything to be perfect for a white Christmas proposal. But just so we're clear, I *did* have my hand on that tree first."

"Do you lie to my sister like that?" I say, kind of joking, kind of serious.

He shakes his head, laughing to himself, and we sit back trying to make sense of where the rest of the conversations have landed.

Shawn arrives a solid two hours after everyone has left and only thirty minutes after the power comes back on. He finds me outside lying down under the large tree in the backyard. The sun is setting, and a real, cool change has finally started to drift through, one that promises to stay. The air smells of summer and BBQ.

"What's going on?"

"Shhh," I say, patting the spot beside me on the deck, "come lie down."

He does so, laying on his back with his hands behind his head.

"Is this not heavenly?"

There's still a hint of warmth to the cool breeze that rustles through the leaves and I find it oddly comforting.

"I reckon just about anywhere with you would be." Shawn turns his head, and our lips meet.

"It's going to take a while to get used to hearing you talk like that to me."

"I can pull it back if—"

"No!" I practically shout, "don't pull anything back. I like it. I'm just not used to it. Ever. From anyone."

I reach my hands out around his neck, drawing him closer to me. His hands cup my face, his thumb runs over my ear. Our lips meet again as though they've been starved of each other for too long, and in this moment, I have no doubt that this will go down as the best Holly Jolly Christmas, ever.

Afterword

The charity mentioned in this book, The Indigenous Literacy Foundation, is a real charity doing important work within remote indigenous communities across Australia. The foundation encourages and supports early literacy in indigenous communities, with a strong focus on providing First Languages books and publishing opportunities to our indigenous communities. Please check out their website at www.indigenousliteracyfoundation. org.au to find out more.

Also by Katie Montinaro

The Girl in the Sunflower Dress

About the Author

Katie Montinaro is Melbourne based romance author. When she's not writing, you'll find her hanging out with her kids, watching movies at the local cinema or designing something for her husband to build. Katie loves to hear from her readers so make sure you stop by her Instagram page (@author_katiemontinaro) and introduce yourself.

For more books and updates head to
www.katiemontinaro.com.au

Made in the USA
Middletown, DE
19 November 2022

15551032R00064